The Wreck
Walker's Guide

KENDALL McDONALD

The Wreck
Walker's Guide

Maps drawn by
SUE LAWES

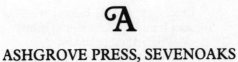

ASHGROVE PRESS, SEVENOAKS

Published in Great Britain by
ASHGROVE PRESS LTD
25 Quakers Hall Lane
Sevenoaks, Kent TN13 3TU

© Kendall McDonald, 1982

ISBN 0 906798 18 3 (hardcover)
ISBN 0 906798 16 7 (paperback)

First published 1982
Photoset in 11/12½ Plantin by
Saildean Limited, Walton-on-Thames
Printed and bound by
The Pitman Press, Bath

CONTENTS

LIST OF ILLUSTRATIONS

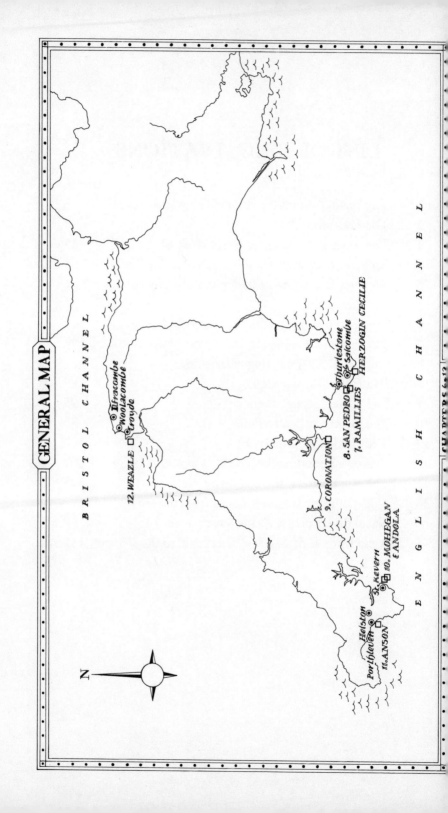

GENERAL MAP

BRISTOL CHANNEL

ENGLISH CHANNEL

N

12. WEAZLE

Ilfracombe
Woolacombe
Croyde

2. CORONATION

Turlestone
8. SAN PEDRO
7. RAMILLIES
Salcombe
HERZOGIN CECILIE

Halston
Porthleven
11. ANSON

5. Kevern
10. MOHEGAN
& ANDOLA

CHAPTERS 6-12

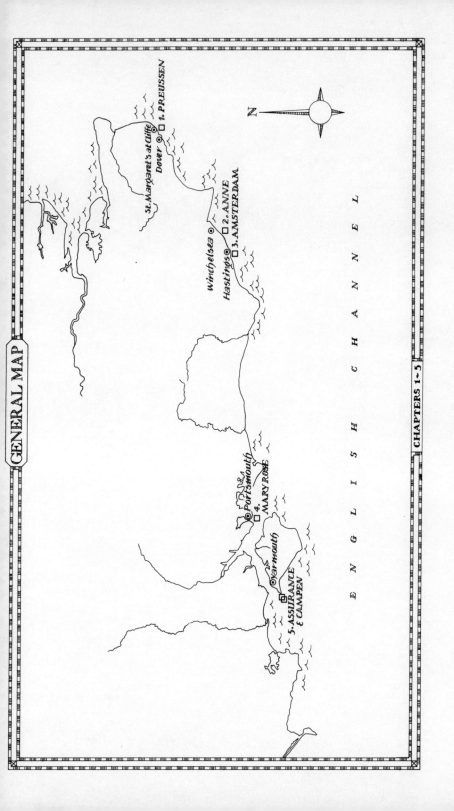

GENERAL MAP

St. Margaret's at Cliffe
Dover ◉ □ 1. PREUSSEN

Winchelsea ◉
Hastings ◉ □ 2. ANNE
□ 3. AMSTERDAM

Portsmouth ◉
□ 4. MARY ROSE

Yarmouth ◉
□ 5. ASSURANCE & CAMPEN

E N G L I S H   C H A N N E L

N

CHAPTERS 1 ~ 5

CHAPTER ONE

Preussen

The date: November 6th, 1910.
The weather: hazy, but with a light breeze, north-by-west, increasing.

The largest sailing ship afloat in the world was about to collide with a cross-Channel ferry. And you can see the wreckage of that great sailing ship today on the black rocks under the White Cliffs of Dover.

The giant German five-master *Preussen* was one of the great racing greyhounds of the seas, the clippers, the four-masted barques, and the five-masted full-riggers, which raced across the world's oceans taking on and often beating the steamers.

They travelled at speeds that even today hardly seem credible – the Yankee clipper *James Baines* held the world record with 21 knots – and they held those speeds, not just in short bursts, but day after day after day. Not that the *Preussen* was racing on the day she was going to die. She was running easily on course from Hamburg to Valparaiso with 5,000 tons of general cargo, and just before midnight she was just eight miles off Newhaven.

The *Preussen* had been built in 1902 and at her launching at Hamburg her tonnage was 4,768 and she was 407 feet 9 inches long and had a beam of 53 feet 7 inches. She was described as a steel ship, which meant that she was steel plated on to steel ribs. The German people, already searching for status symbols, were proud of this great ship. And for eight years the *Preussen* queened it among the world's sailing ships, her tall silhouette towering above most others in the world's larger ports.

Her captain, Heinrich Nissen, had, on that November night, no cause for alarm. True, the sea was becoming perceptibly rougher and the wind was increasing, but the *Preussen* could handle most things that the sea could throw at her. Her crew of 48 were all experienced sailing men. And his passengers were no trouble. There were just two of them – one a painter of seascapes and no stranger to the sea; the other a navigation instructor. What was about to happen made a mockery of navigation!

It was at this moment that Captain Nissen noticed the lights of a steamship on his port side. A quick glance around and aloft told him that his own lights were shining bright. Another look at the steamship told him that the two ships would clear one another easily. But that is where he was terribly wrong.

A minute later and Captain Nissen was suddenly aware that the steamship was very close – much too close. Now he studied the ship carefully and, despite the night, recognised her as one of the Channel ferries. He then made the incredible decision that the steamer must be going astern. Why on earth he should think that any ship should be going astern in mid-Channel, Captain Nissen never made clear. Perhaps he thought that she was giving way to sail. But the ship, which was in fact the *Brighton*, the cross-Channel steamer which plied between Newhaven and Dieppe on the Paris-London service, was not going astern. She came on and on and then, with a grinding crunch, the two ships met.

Captain Nissen watched in horror – in slow-motion it seemed to him then although the *Brighton* was travelling at speed – as his foremast snapped and crashed down with sails still rigged.

On ploughed the *Brighton* into the *Preussen*'s bow. The jib-boom of the sailing ship cracked into matchwood.

In the *Brighton*, it seemed to her Captain that the *Preussen* had loomed up out of the haze from nowhere. And he could be forgiven for thinking at that moment that his ship and her 90 passengers were doomed. For a moment it looked too as

WRECK OF THE 'PREUSSEN'

1 Tugs gather round the stranded *Preussen*, but the end is near

2 The *Preussen* today, at low tide. Eight ribs from the hull near her stern and two more at her bow can be seen

though the *Brighton's* whole deck was going to be swept clean
by the great spars of the *Preussen*. Over the side went her
forward funnel. Her mainmast snapped at the base and joined
the funnel in the sea. Most of her port-side was damaged and
the lifeboats on that side would never save anyone as they were
crushed completely out of boat-shape.

The *Brighton* swept on. Her after-funnel took a savage blow,
but though dislodged remained aboard. Her Captain ordered
"Stop engines" but resisted the desire to go astern, and his ship
wallowed to a stop within hailing distance of the other.
Everyone kept their heads and a quick survey of the damage
showed that the *Preussen* had come off worst and was taking in
water from the damage to her bow.

Once the Captain of the *Brighton* realised that he was in no
danger of sinking he stood by the sailing ship until it was clear
that the weather was deteriorating, a gale was coming up out of
the darkness and blowing directly on to the English shore. The
seas too were rising and the *Brighton's* passengers were the
Captain's first concern. He turned back for Newhaven.

The *Brighton* reached the port at about three in the morning
and the London and Brighton Railway Company's tug *Alert*
was sent to help the *Preussen*. The steamer's shaken passengers
– those who wanted to continue their journey to France –
were transferred, together with the mails and their baggage,
to the French cross-Channel steamer *France*. The Captain of
the *Brighton* made a simple report to his employers – that he
had been steering north-north-west off Newhaven when he
came into collision with the five-masted sailing ship *Preussen*.
To this brief report he added his provisional estimate of the
damage to both ships. He did not mention whose fault he considered the accident to be and even today it is not clear
who was responsible. Both Captains were cleared in their own
countries.

Out in the darkness at sea Captain Nissen was still hove-to,
trying to stem the leaks in the fore-peak and at the same time
clear away the wreckage. He expected the tug that the *Brighton*
had promised to send, but when nothing appeared, he decided
to make for Portsmouth. He soon had to abandon this plan as

the wind backed more to the westward. Now he decided to try for Dover. But this was by no means easy. The wind increased so much that when passing Dungeness he had to seek shelter in East Bay.

At that moment Captain Nissen saw a very comforting sight. Out of the dark came the tug *Albatross*, which had beaten the *Alert* in the hunt for the stricken ship. As the tug came close enough to hail he asked her skipper for his advice on where to anchor. Once he had that advice he followed it and ordered the starboard anchor away. But no sooner had the chain started to run out than a squall hit the *Preussen*. The chain shot out in jerks and within seconds 90 fathoms of it had screamed to the seabed. Captain Nissen immediately ordered out the port anchor to take the strain which was bound to come. But it was too late and the starboard anchor chain snapped like a piece of string.

Captain Nissen yelled for the port anchor to be taken up, but again it was too late and the port chain parted in the same manner. With both anchors gone, Nissen put *Preussen* on to the starboard tack and hove-to as best he could. Now the tug *Albatross* came right alongside and Nissen decided to make for home. Would the tug tow him there? The skipper of the *Albatross* had grave doubts about it. He didn't like the look of the weather at all. The decision was shelved however, for the Dover pilot cutter *Pathfinder*, with John Dickson, the Trinity House pilot, aboard, also came alongside the *Preussen*. John Dickson had no doubts. The glass was falling rapidly, and he was sure it was too dangerous to take the ship right across the North Sea. The only thing to do was to engage more tugs and make for Dover. Nissen agreed. But they didn't need to call for tugs. They arrived almost as though they scented work. One of them was the *Alert*, which was made fast on the starboard side amidships. The *John Bull* took the starboard bow and the *Albatross* the port. Then they got under way. Destination Dover.

At first it went well, despite the increasing seas and wind. From being a Force Four when Nissen had tried to anchor, the squalls had changed into a continuous blow of Force Six and increasing. Nissen had only one shred of comfort in this stage of his fight against the sea - that in the collision no one had been hurt. The master of the *Alert* had told him this. "Thank God for that", said Nissen, and turned back to his charts.

From those charts he could see that safety was not all that far away. They were making a good seven knots and the only thing that Nissen could see of two of the tugs were the towing wires leading away into the dark. *John Bull* had 60 fathoms of four-inch wire out and the *Albatross* 120 fathoms of five-inch. They rounded towards Dover Harbour, but the wind increased to Force Eight, to Force Nine. The seas were huge and squalls ripped in from the direction of Dungeness.

It was now four in the morning and still dark, so Captain Nissen was glad to have John Dickson at his side. Dickson was giving the orders as pilot, and though the cross-seas were making steering difficult, the tugs were winning their way towards the eastern entrance to the harbour.

Nissen's spirits lifted. The water was being held by the pumps. All the wreckage had been cleared away, though the *Preussen's* 80-foot-long steel bowsprit was bent to port like a banana. He knew that if they could get her into harbour she could be repaired. But his luck changed again.

Suddenly the tugs were making no headway. The wind and tide had them. However hard the tugs strained, and the towing wires were taut like bow-strings, they could not move her. The only thing they could do now was to pull her head to sea. Both Nissen and Dickson agreed that the best thing now was for the *Preussen* to make sail and try and ride the wind out at sea.

The command had no sooner been given and *Alert* started to cast off than the *John Bull's* tow-wire snapped. Captain Nissen saw what was going to happen. He yelled for the lower topsails to be set in an effort to back her off, but the *Preussen*, hit by yet another squall solid with rain and spray, in John Dickson's words "walked away from the tugs". More wires snapped and the *Preussen* was free. Free, but helpless.

It was now dawn and they could see, but there was little that could be done to help her. Two tugs were soon lying to seaward and two more moved out from Dover Harbour.

Comforting sight though it was, Captain Nissen knew that it wouldn't be long before he went aground under those great white cliffs. But he fought with every trick he had learned in all his sailing years to edge out just a little from the white wall of chalk. First one tug and then another tried to get lines to him, but every attempt failed.

In Dover there was no doubt that she was going to strike and that belief was made clear when the first maroon exploded over the town calling the lifeboatmen and rocket-line crews to their stations. As more maroons soared skywards, their explosions sounded muted among the clouds and rain, but boatmen and seamen heard them clearly enough and came hurrying to the lifeboat station on the marine promenade. The lifeboat *Mary Hamar Hoyle* was ready and Coxwain Brockman picked his men carefully. He knew that once clear of the harbour's shelter the lifeboat would be in for a savage battering by the enormous seas.

Even so, one of the volunteers who was told to take a seat was James Driscoll, who was over sixty. Brockman thought his knowledge and experience would be worth more than the brawn of some younger man. Dozens of willing hands seized the hauling-off rope and heaved, but the lifeboat stuck. Another more concerted heave and the boat slid forward and plunged into the sea. Another maroon was fired to tell the *Preussen* that help was on its way and this performed a dual purpose, for one of the Dover tugs came back and took the lifeboat in tow.

That maroon struck a death-knell too for the *Preussen*. Captain Nissen heard it, but he knew that his ship was lost. Louder than the sound of the maroon was the crunch as the great ship hit the rocks of Fan Point.

Up on the cliffs, the St. Margaret's rocket-apparatus crew struggled with their gear through winds that made standing difficult and threatened to hurl them all over the cliffs into the sea. It wasn't until they fought their way down into the comparative shelter of the great depression they call Fan Hole that they could hear one another speak. And almost right below them they could see *Preussen*, her masts nearly reaching up towards them.

Though they had no difficulty in making the ship out, Coastguard Arthur Hughes had his doubts about the possibility of getting a line across her in the face of the wind which was blowing directly on shore. The tide was rising and nothing could save the ship, but even if a line could be dropped across the ship, hauling the crew up to the cliff in the breeches-buoy would be a dangerous job. He didn't much fancy the chances of the lifeboat either. Any attempt to go alongside would mean being dashed against her – she was broadside on to the shore and the wind now – and there looked little room inside her, each new wave was bumping her across the hidden rocks to the actual face of the cliff.

In the lifeboat, Coxwain Brockman was thinking the same. Gradually, as the tug pulled the lifeboat nearer and nearer to the stricken ship, Brockman could see that the *Preussen* had struck all right. Somehow – shouting was no use as the words were whipped away by the wind as soon as they were spoken – Brockman and the skipper of the tug *Lady Vita* worked together. While the tug held station off, the lifeboat was "lowered" on the end of a long hawser to the *Preussen*.

As they neared the ship, the lifeboat crew shouted in unison, but there was no reply. One moment the ship towered over them, then as they were lifted by giant waves the deck was almost below them. There was no sign of life and the lack of movement struck Brockman as eerie. Lights burned in the deckhouse, but there was no sign of anyone, nor any reply to further shouts.

Suddenly a huge wave broke against the *Preussen*. The lifeboatmen could hear the crunch as she bottomed hard. The same wave swamped the lifeboat and when it had passed, Brockman seeing his crew sitting nearly up to their waists in water, decided it was time to go. The tug towed them off and finally they got safely back into harbour.

By 10.30 that night a second rocket-apparatus crew were in position. These were the Dover coastguards and they had struggled along the foot of the cliffs. Communication between the two teams was essential. One could spoil the other's efforts, so Arthur Hughes climbed down a rope ladder from the cliffs at the low part of Fan Hole to the foreshore.

It was a perilous climb as the rope ladder span in the gale, cutting his hands against the cliff and to his horror the ladder ended 30 feet above the shore. But with his lifeline he slid down the rest of the way using his injured hands to push himself off the cliff.

Once on the shore, he could hear the *Preussen* grinding with each wave. She was now only 200 yards out. The lights still burned amidships, but the rest of the ship was dark. But the rocket crews could see her clearly – each sweep of the South Foreland lighthouse, only a mile away along the cliffs, lit her up like a ghost ship.

Aboard *Preussen* there were no ghosts. Captain Nissen, his passengers and crew were very much alive. All hands took turns at the pumps and they sang softly as they worked. Sang softly, so that they could hear clearly the bumping and grinding from beneath their feet and work out just how much damage the rocks of Fan Point were doing to the ship. They were reasonably comfortable. Food and hot drinks were on hand and so high were the sides of the *Preussen* that not all that much sea came aboard.

The men on board were, in fact, much more comfortable than those outside intent on saving them. But suddenly there was a change for the worse. There was a rush of water into the forward hold and despite increased efforts on the pumps, the water rose to fourteen feet. Captain Nissen was sure some other part of the ship was giving way and ordered distress signals to be fired.

At 11 p.m. the watchers saw the distress rockets and the lifeboat was launched again. At last the wind seemed to be dropping. Now the *Preussen* seemed to be more over on her side. A rocket-line dropped across her, but the German sailors refused to use the breeches-buoy. The Dover lifeboat didn't have any better luck. When they got within range a few shouted sentences told the tired lifeboat crew that the *Preussen* crew intended to stay with their ship as long as there was any chance of her being saved. Nissen had obviously changed his

mind. The lifeboatmen muttered obscenities. They could understand the crew's feelings, but did the Germans understand
their's, sitting in an open boat for hours at a time! Another
rocket line came across the ship from the shore, but it made no
difference. They were not leaving the ship.

Came the dawn and the watchers on the shore could hear the
Germans singing louder. At first they had difficulty in recog-
nising the song. Then with the wind behind it came a
full-blooded chorus of the sea-shanty "Away Rio". But soon
the mood changed and the concertina accompaniment was
clearly that of a hymn. The lifeboat crew left and once again
smashed through the teeth of the seas to harbour. Those seas
had done more damage to the *Preussen*. Her bowsprit was gone.
So was more of the fore-mast. Tugs came and went. At one
time there were ten in attendance, but the *Preussen* was so hard
on that nothing could move her.

At 9 a.m. the lifeboat took station again, but nothing would
persuade the men to leave. In the *Preussen* they just pointed to
the ship and indicated that they were staying aboard. They
lowered a bottle of brandy into the lifeboat, but that was the
only thing that left the ship. In the afternoon the lifeboat came
back into harbour. The men were so cold and tired that no one
could even summon up enough strength to throw a line ashore.
When they left the boat they could hardly walk, but that
sixty-year-old James Driscoll said: "We'll go out again if they
want us".

At last, however, one man did leave the *Preussen*. Ashore in a
small boat came Captain Nissen to talk to the agents of the
owner, Ferdinand Laeisz. Once ashore it was too rough for him
to get back, but he planned to return the next day.

By now most of the country knew of *Preussen's* fight for
survival. Crowds of sightseers made their way to Dover and up
on to the cliffs to look down on the wrecked ship. The Press, of
course, kept up running reports of the story and an enterprising
Daily Mail reporter managed to get a short interview with
Captain Nissen. Said he:

"When I sighted the *Brighton* I thought she was going
astern, but somehow we collided.

"I am proud of my men. When the lifeboat came to us they said to me, 'Captain, we will stick by you. At worst, we can swim ashore and we have lifebelts'. They were cheerful, and they sang the night through at the pumps as they worked. They did not mind and we were fairly comfortable, although she lifted and bumped heavily, but not much sea came aboard, for my ship is high. Even the passengers did not mind, and when I came off they decided to remain in the ship. They are brave fellows.

"I want to be back with them tonight, but no boat can put me aboard. Tomorrow I go back, and I hope then to get my ship off and have her pumped clear".

Brave words, but it seems unlikely that even Captain Nissen believed them. It was common knowledge that she had fourteen feet of water in her hold, held back only by constant pumping. There was a great hole in the bow and it looked as though the bows themselves had been partly torn from the hull. The only thing in her favour was that the wind was now moderating fast, though the seas were taking longer to go down and that night her hull was a black shape in an ocean of foam.

The *Preussen* was finished. That became clear when November 9th dawned fine and clear and Captain Nissen assembled his crew on the sloping deck of that once great ship. He had a last duty to perform. While ashore at the office of his agents he had received a telegram from Germany. It was from the Kaiser. He read it to them:

"Deeply moved by the news of the disaster to the proud five-master *Preussen*, I desire to express to the owners my warmest sympathy. I should like a direct report regarding the result of the catastrophe and especially about the fate of the brave crew, which causes me much anxiety".

When he had finished, Captain Heinrich Nissen looked at his crew in silence for a moment. Then, taking off his cap, he called for "Three cheers for the Emperor". Then, leaving only a skeleton watch on board, he, the rest of the crew and the passengers came ashore. They told enquirers that the *Preussen* was hull-pierced in two places as well as the damage to her bows. It was over and salvage work on her cargo started immediately.

The *Preussen* took a long time for the sea to break her up and she was still recognisable a year later when, on March 4th, 1911, Mr. Justice Bargrave Deane, sitting with two of the Elder Brethren of Trinity House, was called on to decide a damage action brought by the *Preussen* owner, Ferdinand Laeisz against the London, Brighton and South Coast Railway Company, who admitted that the collision was caused by the negligent navigation of the *Brighton*.

They denied, however, that the later stranding was a result of the collision!

On April 12th, Mr. Justice Bargrave Deane gave judgment for Laeisz, finding that the stranding was a direct result of the collision, and that the Railway Company was responsible for the whole loss. On November 20th, the claims came before the Admiralty Registrar. The claim for the *Preussen* herself was £52,000. The cargo was valued at £22,000. But nobody got anything like that for the Railway Company had paid into court £8,761 as the limit of their liability for all claims.

There the matter rested, but one of the most amazing things about the story of the *Preussen* is that you can still see her today. At low tide up from the seabed come eight of her ribs from her hull near the stern and two more at her bow. After over 70 years the sea has still not destroyed her completely.

How to get there

This is a most beautiful walk along the top of the White Cliffs of Dover. The approach depends on how far you wish to walk. The longest route starts just behind the entrance to Dover's Eastern Docks, from which most of the car-ferries leave for the Continent. Parking at busy times and the high season can be a problem here. If you are lucky you can leave your car on the

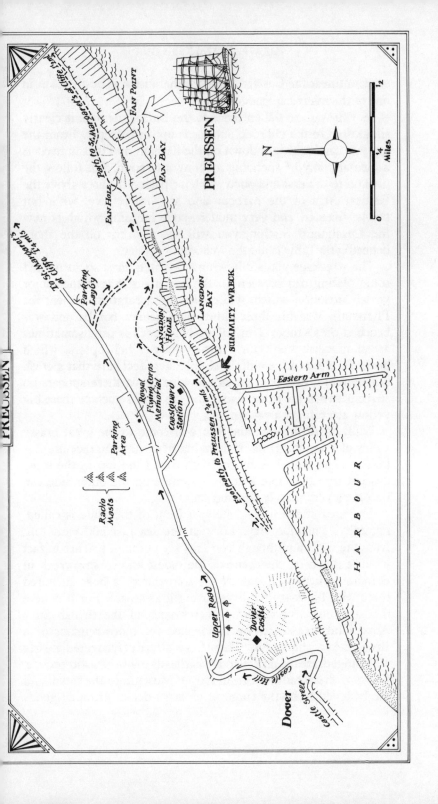

sea front near the Eastern Docks. Otherwise it is best to park in one of the many car-parks nearby.

As you walk to the entrance to the Docks, the path is clearly signposted to the cliff-top and leads upward steeply. From the top you can look right down on the harbour and that in itself is a pleasant way of spending a sunny afternoon. But follow the path on to the east and once you have passed the area above the Eastern Arm of the harbour and are almost level with, but below, the new and very modern-style building which is now the Coastguard Station, you will see a wreck on the shore beneath you. This is *not* the *Preussen*.

The wreckage you are looking at - a steel mast sticks up and some plating can be seen on the beach - is that of the motor vessel *Summity*, which, while carrying a cargo of cement for Plymouth, was hit three times by German bombs and was beached on October 27th, 1940. The wreck is used sometimes as an exercise mark for Air-Sea Rescue helicopters, which hover so close to the cliffs that onlookers feel sure that a crash is inevitable. But even though looking down there appears no space between the rotor blades and the cliff, somehow these big yellow aircraft get away with it.

Walk on to the east and you will come to the great grassy valley of Langdon Hole. If there has been any rain recently it is best to skirt the Hole by the path round the top as the steep descent into the Hole and the scramble up the other side can become a very muddy slip and slide.

The area at sea immediately in front of the Hole is called, naturally, Langdon Bay. Look at the sea just 500 yards out from the cliffs and though you may see nothing, you are in fact looking down on the scene of the oldest known shipwreck in Britain. You may, however, see something - a boat anchored there with black-suited divers using it as a base. For it is here that amateur divers from Dover branch of the British Sub-Aqua Club are searching the seabed for more remains of a Bronze Age shipwreck. They have already recovered nearly 100 winged axes, daggers and spearheads made of solid bronze. Some of these can be seen in Dover Museum in the town, and are believed to be the cargo of an arms-dealer bringing goods to Britain from the Continent sometime around 1200-1000 B.C.

Follow the cliff path onwards and very soon all traces of civilisation disappear. In summer, the long grass is a favourite haunt of skylarks which track great singing circles in the sky around you. The path is now diverted slightly inland at a sign "Danger. Cliff Fall", but returns to the edge of the cliff as soon as the area which is sinking away is safely past.

Soon another great grassy pit appears before you. This is Fan Hole and the remains of the *Preussen* are just below the point on the opposite side. This is Fan Point, and because you have timed your visit to coincide with low tide, you will be able to sea clearly those black steel ribs sticking up out of the sea. There are eight at the stern and then two more mark the bow area. Take care at the Point and keep well away from the edge. The grass can be slippery and on windy days eddies can be dangerous. Remember you are 246 feet above the sea and the cliff is sheer.

On a good day Fan Hole is an absolute sun-trap and is a good spot to picnic. The route down is roughly stepped by other walkers' feet, but once again is extremely slippery after rain. It is quite a slog up the other side to Fan Point.

It is interesting to go down into the grassy bowl of Fan Hole as it is here that the St. Margaret's rocket-line team set up their apparatus and shot a line across the *Preussen* all those years ago.

It is over the edge of the smaller but still sheer cliff at the foot of the hole that Coastguard Arthur Hughes clambered on a rope ladder to make contact with the Dover rocket team on the rocks below. Don't go too close to the edge as long grass covers it, concealing the actual start of the sheer drop.

It is just under two miles from the start of the footpath to the grave of the *Preussen* by this route. Those who want a shorter walk should drive from the centre of Dover following the signs for "Dover Castle".

These signs will take you along Castle Street and up the winding hill towards the Castle. Go on past the Castle entrance and after a very steep bend where there is a special parking area for coaches, look out for a sharp turn to the right marked

"Langdon Cliffs and St. Margaret's Bay". This is in fact Upper Road and runs along the cliffs – but not so close that you can see them – to the pretty village of St. Margaret at Cliffe.

Carry on past the entrance to the Coastguard Station and when you are just about level with four huge radio masts on your left, there is a gravelled turning on your left. This leads to a tarmaced area which is often used by learner drivers to get their first feel of a car, but which provides plenty of parking space for our purpose.

You will see foundations of old huts and almost in the centre on the side closest to the road is a memorial stone. It tells you simply that it was from this field that No. 2, 3, 4 and 5 Squadrons of the Royal Flying Corps left on 13-15th August, 1914 for Amiens and the air battles of World War One. It is interesting to note that not far away, closer to the Castle, is a memorial to Bleriot's historic first flight across the Channel.

Having parked, walk 500 yards further down the road until you see an easy entrance and wide track on the right hand side by a small lay-by. This is not a real lay-by, but it is possible for three or four cars to park here just off the road itself. The spaces are usually taken. From here a wide track leads you to the cliffs between Langdon Hole and Fan Hole, and makes the trip to the *Preussen* just a long stroll.

To make sure of arriving at the *Preussen* site at low tide, look in your newspaper for the times of high water at London Bridge. Then subtract 2 hours 42 minutes to give you high tide at Dover. To this add 6 hours and you will get a rough time for low tide on the *Preussen*.

CHAPTER TWO

Anne

The date: July 4th, 1690.
The weather: sea calm, light breezes.

An English 70-gun ship of the line was about to be beached to save her from capture by the French.

The Battle of Beachy Head had started badly on June 30th, had gone badly and finished, for the English, so badly that London gossips said that "the Dutch had the honour, the French the advantage, and the English the shame". Part of the shame of the English was the beaching and setting on fire of the 70-gun ship, the *Anne*, in Rye Bay.

The *Anne* was a fine ship. She was launched at Chatham in 1678 and was built to the design of Phineas Pett, who supervised her construction himself. Just two inches short of 151 feet long, her beam was 40 feet, and in those great wooden walls she carried twenty-six 32-pounder cannon on her main deck, twenty-six 12-pounders on the upper deck, ten 6-pounders, called sakers, on the quarter-deck and four more on the forecastle. Four 3-pounders guarded her poop. She carried 460 men. But all those guns could not save her.

During the Battle of Beachy Head – the Defeat of Beachy Head would be a better title – the *Anne*, commanded by Captain John Tyrrell, was in the rear squadron, the Blue, under Vice Admiral Sir Ralph Delavall, who flew his flag in *Coronation*, which was to survive only a year longer than the

Anne (See Chapter 9). The whole English fleet was commanded by Arthur Herbert, Earl of Torrington.

Not a command to be envied, for Torrington was outnumbered by the French, who had nearly 70 ships to his 56. The French Admiral, the Comte de Tourville, led his ships out of Brest and worked his way up the Channel with the intention of blockading the Thames. The two fleets sighted one another on June 25th, and Torrington withdrew slowly up the Channel, not wanting to fight until he was reinforced. Those reinforcements never arrived and on June 29th he could go on skirmishing no longer. Orders from Queen Mary and the Council in London ordered him to fight. And at 8 a.m. on June 30th, with Beachy Head only four leagues to the north-west, the battle began.

The Dutch ships were in the lead and were in action within the hour. They fought well and bravely, but were caught between the fire of the main French fleet and other French ships which had managed to double round behind them. Then, as the French were in a crescent-moon formation, the Blue squadron of the English were heavily engaged, but Torrington and his squadron in the middle of the line could only fire at long range. The *Anne* found herself fighting French ships by 9.30 a.m. Under Admiral Delavall's orders, she bore down on the French with a strong breeze behind her, but did not open fire until she was at musket shot distance from the enemy.

The French didn't care for this close encounter work and kept edging away. At 2 p.m. the breeze dropped and the ships of the Blue now found themselves becalmed and in the middle of a slugging match. "Very hot" was the description of the Blue squadron's battle at this stage and one captain said that "the enemy shot went through and through ... had six feet of water in the hold and with great difficulty towed off and stopt her leeks". Whether this captain was John Tyrrell of the *Anne* we don't know but when action was broken off at 4 p.m., the *Anne* was badly hurt.

So badly damaged was she that she had to be towed out of danger into the middle of the allied fleet.

On July 1st, Torrington held a council of war. There was no

STATUTORY INSTRUMENTS

1974 No. 910

PROTECTION OF WRECKS

The Protection of Wrecks (Designation No. 7) Order 1974

Made - - -	23rd *May* 1974
Laid before Parliament	30th *May* 1974
Coming into Operation	20th *June* 1974

The Secretary of State, being satisfied that the site identified in article 2 of this Order is the site of a vessel lying wrecked on the sea bed and that on account of the historical and archaeological importance of the vessel the site ought to be protected from unauthorised interference, after consulting with the persons referred to in section 1(4) of the Protection of Wrecks Act 1973(a), in exercise of the powers conferred on him by section 1(1), (2) and (4) of that Act and of all other powers enabling him in that behalf hereby orders as follows:

1.—(1) This Order may be cited as the Protection of Wrecks (Designation No. 7) Order 1974 and shall come into operation on 20th June 1974.

(2) The Interpretation Act 1889(b) shall apply to the interpretation of this Order as it applies to the interpretation of an Act of Parliament.

2. The site in respect of which this Order is made is hereby identified as the site where the vessel HMS "Anne" lies wrecked on the sea bed at Latitude 50° 53′ 22″ North, Longitude 00° 41′ 46″ East.

3. The area within a distance of 75 metres of Latitude 50° 53′ 22″ North, Longitude 00° 41′ 46″ East shall be a restricted area for the purposes of the Protection of Wrecks Act 1973.

23rd May 1974.

> *S. C. Davis,*
> Parliamentary Under Secretary of State
> for Companies, Aviation and Shipping,
> Department of Trade.

(a) 1973 c. 33.   (b) 1889 c. 63.

3   The order protecting the wreck of *H.M.S. Anne*

choice. The French had lost no ships at all. The English and Dutch had lost, or looked like losing due to the damage to them, seven ships. So Torrington decided to retreat. Any ships which could not keep up were to be abandoned.

But Captain John Tyrrell did not like this at all and rather than abandon his *Anne* to certain capture, he wallowed along behind the main fleet. The French, oddly enough in view of their lack of losses, did not seem keen to pounce on such a straggler. Seeing Tyrrell's troubles, the captains of both the *York* and the *Swallow*, who were his personal friends, came back and, at great risk to their own ships, gave the *Anne* a tow. Finally, however, they had to abandon the towlines and rejoin the main fleet. Tyrrell struggled on alone.

By July 3rd, the *Anne* was dropping further and further back and Captain Tyrrell took no comfort from the sight of four badly damaged Dutch ships being scuttled or burned near Hastings.

The next day the *Anne* was even further behind and her position was hopeless. Captain Tyrrell fired a gun to attract attention to his plight and Torrington sent his yacht back to find out what the gun meant. Tyrrell sent a message to the Admiral that unless his ship could be protected she was in danger of being captured. Torrington replied that no help could be given. Tyrrell had fought a good fight and now he knew what he had to do. The *Anne* altered course and slowly made her way inshore.

The French were closer now, scenting an easy kill, but Tyrrell still had time to select his spot for beaching. He chose well and the *Anne* slid to a halt on a deep mud beach midway between Hastings and Rye, close to the little hamlet of Pett Level. Everything that was reasonably portable was taken out of her and the next day when the French looked as though they were about to land troops to loot what was left, the *Anne* was set on fire.

A contemporary report of the time records it like this:

"Saturday 5th July ... This afternoon the *Anne* Frigat was set on fire, we not being able to help her any longer after the French came up with her. She was ashore the day before in

Rye Bay, and we have saved most of her trade except her guns which will be taken up again".

As the *Anne* guttered and hissed into steam where the fire met the water, the allied fleet escaped from Admiral Tourville. Torrington was court-martialled, acquitted, but never given a command again.

So what was left of the *Anne* was abandoned and forgotten except by the curious who noted the outline of a great ship in the mud whenever exceptionally low tides came to the area. And she would have remained forgotten if it had not been for the sudden interest in the 1970s in marine archaeology – and the fact that some people, perhaps spurred on by the story of the *Amsterdam* at Hastings (see next chapter), took a bulldozer down to the wreck site to see what they could find. And they found a surprising amount – iron cannon balls, grenades, lead musket balls, wooden barrels, clay pipes, a spoon and a pewter plate. Their discoveries were reported in the local press and the archaeologists reacted at once.

The *Anne* was made a "protected historic wreck" and now it is against the law to disturb her. The archaeologists believe that the bottom 6 feet of the ship's hull lies under the mud on a bed of firm clay and is just on the low tide mark. They believe that she should be preserved for a proper archaeological excavation because some items still there under the mud can tell us a great deal not just about the construction of ships of long ago, but also about her armament and the use of the ship.

How to get there

From Hastings take the A259 and turn off to the right at signs for "Fairlight". Now a winding road takes you through beautiful countryside – including a special viewing point at Fairlight from which you can see much of the coast and country to the east. Continue on and you will come to the little hamlet of Pett Level. Go past the village stores taking care at a sharp turn to the left. Almost immediately on your right is a public house called, appropriately in view of the history of this area, The Smuggler. This cheery pub is snuggled down behind the sea wall which protects this section of the land, and the landlord will show you the Admiralty chart with the site of the wreck marked clearly as being protected under the Protection of Wrecks Act 1973.

Park opposite the pub. You can walk through to the left of the pub as you face it and up some steps to the top of the sea wall. This is stoutly made with the side to the sea faced with paving stones well bitumened into place.

This section of the top of the sea wall is a wide walkway to your left. To your right as you face out to sea at the end of the beach are the low cliffs called naturally enough "Cliff End". They are National Trust property. All the beach to your left is backed by the sea wall and the small shingle and sand/mud beach is laced with many wooden groynes to save the sand being washed away and to help stop the flooding of the low ground behind the sea wall.

The sea wall is our path to the wreck site. Walk along it to your left past the houses which shelter behind it and on to which you look down. Go on past the New Beach Club and at the end of the houses the path along the top of the wall narrows to a single track. We are getting close now. Looking along the coast ahead of us to the east you can see the famous Camber Sands and out over Romney Marsh. On the horizon two lighthouses and the nuclear power station mark the tip of the desolate Dungeness promontory. The nuclear power station is open to visitors on Wednesday afternoons in the summer and that and the vast Bird Sanctuary make an interesting drive after visiting the wreck of the *Anne*. But please note that you need a permit to visit the bird sanctuary, and this should be obtained in advance from the Royal Society for the Protection of Birds, The Lodge, Sandy, Bedfordshire.

To pinpoint the wreck site of the *Anne* you should walk along the narrow path on the top of the sea wall past two sets of

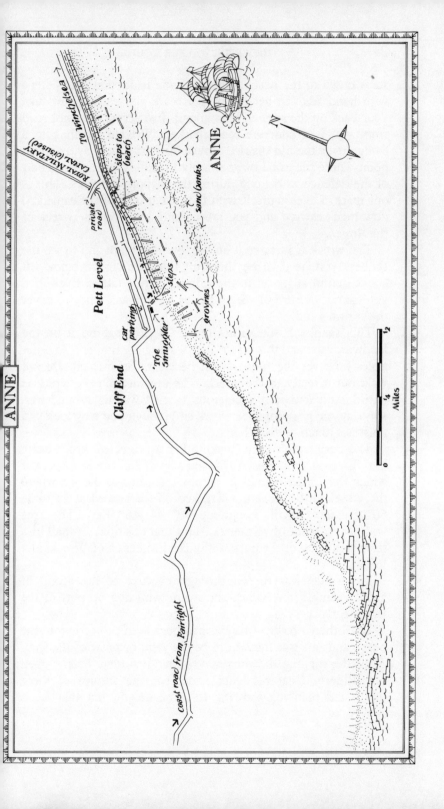

steps down to the beach. Ahead of you is another set of steps with handrails. To get the proper mark you should now turn your back on the sea and look inland. Just across the coast road from you is a concrete road marked "Private" leading to a bridge over the old disused Royal Military Canal at the exact point where the canal turns sharply inland. The canal was part of the defence works dug during the Napoleonic wars. This is our mark. Level yourself with the inland turn of the canal and now turn seaward and you are looking out over the wreck of the *Anne*.

The wreck is just about on the low-tide mark and to see the timbers you need to be there on tides which are below 2ft above datum at Dover in the Admiralty tide tables. Even then you cannot be sure of seeing her as a sandbank tends to cover the seaward end.

This sandbank sometimes creates a pool behind it on the landward side and this water may obscure the timbers. At other times however the timbers can be clear. Be warned. Do not walk out directly to the wreck. The area around the wreck is liquid mud and it is dangerous to risk wading around her. Anyway she is a protected wreck and though you may look you must not touch or disturb her.

The designation order making her a protected wreck came into force on June 20th, 1974, and says: "The site in respect of which this Order is made is hereby identified as the site where the vessel HMS *Anne* lies wrecked on the seabed at Latitude 50° 53' 22" North, Longitude 00° 41' 46" East. The area within a distance of 75 metres ... (of that position) ... shall be a restricted area for the purposes of the Protection of Wrecks Act 1973".

The order was rushed through because of the group of people using a mechanical excavator who dug up part of the wreck early in 1974.

Until then a piece of timber had been seen projecting up the beach and this was thought to be the stem or prow of the ship. After the digging the timber was found to have been ripped out. Elderly local residents remember the stumps of three masts and planking showing to some height, but that is no longer the case. There is no doubt though that the whole of the ship's bottom survives as well as many of her ribs. Some of the variety of objects found by the diggers – iron cannon balls, grenades, musket balls, clay pipes, spoons, pieces of wooden barrels and a pewter plate were handed in to Portsmouth Museum but much disappeared.

CHAPTER THREE

Amsterdam

The date: Sunday, January 26th, 1749.
The weather: leaden skies, rain squalls, south-westerly gale.

A giant Dutch East Indiaman, en route from the Zuider Zee to Batavia, rudderless and with a mutinous crew aboard, was about to end her first and only voyage on the beach near Hastings, Sussex. And the looting was about to begin ...

But that voyage of the *Amsterdam* had really started back in November the previous year, shortly after she was launched. Put in command was Captain Willem Klump. Captain Klump was 33 and this was his second command. Despite his youth he was obviously highly thought of as the *Amsterdam* was one of the largest of the types of East Indiamen. She was a 700-ton ship, 150 feet long and with a beam of 35 feet. Like all the ships of the Dutch East India Company, she was heavily armed to defend her valuable cargo. Fifty-four cannon were deployed on two main gun decks.

She had been built in the Company's own shipyards in Amsterdam under an early system of "automation" by means of which ship parts were mass-produced and were interchangeable.

The *Amsterdam* had taken exactly four months to build - a similar ship in British dockyards took at least a year and often two! But there was no scrimping or corner-cutting to save money. The ship was built to last. The East Indiamen had to be as some voyages took over a year for just the outward trip.

4   Archaelogists study the *Amsterdam* at low tide

Captain Klump inspected his ship and was pleased with what he saw. His crew must have pleased him less. Seamen who were prepared to sign on for such long runs were often the dregs of humanity. Some, he noted, were still sun-tanned from a previous voyage, which meant that they had spent their pay in a few short weeks on whores and drink and now had no alternative but to go back to sea. Some were, Klump suspected, unwell, but if a man could walk up the gang-plank and the Company had signed him on, then there was little he could do about it. One man actually died as soon as he joined the *Amsterdam* and before she even sailed!

This sort of thing hardly worried the Dutch East India Company, the Vereenigde Oostindische Compagnie, whose intertwined initials VOC appeared on a lot more than the cannons of their ships. For the VOC was the most powerful single commercial operation that the world has ever known, bigger by far than the modern Shell or BP, General Motors or Ford, or Mitsubishi, ICI, or any other great trading name in the world today.

In fact, the VOC was richer and stronger than many nations of its time. Its trading empire stretched from the Cape of Good Hope, to India, Ceylon, Sumatra, Java, the Celebes and Spice Islands, and the ports of Malaya, China and Japan. It was authorised by the Dutch Government to make war if it thought it necessary, to build forts, villages, towns, cities. It had its own law, even its own ministers of religion.

The ships flying the red, white and blue flag of Holland carried the bulk of cargoes in home waters and most of the spice and other treasure from the East. The biggest herring and whaling fleets were Dutch. Amsterdam was the banking capital of the world – and the reason for all this was the prosperity of the VOC.

Klump and the *Amsterdam* were just one cog in that great operation, though perhaps he didn't see it like that. In fact his first task was to make sure that his ship was ready to sail with the "Autumn" fleet from Amsterdam that November in 1748.

The VOC tried to organise its voyages to the East Indies into two fleets for security reasons. One sailed in the Spring

and one in the Autumn. And Klump made it with the Autumn
fleet. On board there were 329 men, one-third of them soldiers
for duty in Batavia, and three women passengers. In her holds
were thousands of bottles of French wine and other goods.
There too, in the Captain's quarters, were 24 chests of
wedge-shaped silver bars and four chests containing 16,000
silver ducatoons. These were being sent to Batavia, which is
now Djakarta, so that company officials could buy goods for
shipment back to Holland.

On November 15th, with a nice steady easterly wind behind
her the *Amsterdam* set off into the North Sea with 12,000 miles
of voyaging ahead of her. But it didn't work out like that.
Suddenly the wind swung to the north-west. Klump anchored
rather than be blown on shore. For four days they rode out the
most appalling weather and then, seizing his chance in a
comparative lull, Klump brought the *Amsterdam* back into
Texel. Two days later the wind swung easterly again and
Klump had another go.

Within a short time the wind swung to the north-west once
again and he was pinned down again by an on-shore wind. It
took two weeks this time before he could get back to an
anchorage at Texel and there he waited. And waited. It was a
period of sheer frustration for all aboard. For Klump allowed
no one but himself or his officers ashore and conditions below
decks in the cold and wet grew worse and worse without sea
breezes to blow through the ship. One man died, but he had
probably been ill long before he came aboard. Klump used his
crew during this long wait to make adjustments to the new
ship's rigging which the earlier storms had shown to be
necessary. Even at Christmas the crew stayed aboard and so
did the soldiers. Klump probably cannot be blamed for this
seeming inhumanity – the food and wines in his quarters were
no doubt excellent – because there is little doubt that if he had
let any men ashore he would never have seen them again.

Finally, the storms passed and the wind settled in the east
and Klump got the *Amsterdam* out of the Zuider Zee for the
third and last time on January 8th, 1749. It wasn't third time
lucky. The *Amsterdam* was hit by one of the worst south-

westerly gales recorded for the North Sea. But she had gone too far to turn back this time.

One of the VOC ships which had sailed the day before *Amsterdam* ran ashore between Eastney Point and Southsea Castle. Ships raced for shelter anywhere they could. Sea defences collapsed and land flooded. The wind went on and on. Out at sea Captain Klump tacked and tacked. Mountainous seas hampered each change of sails. Men were swept overboard, but that wasn't Klump's greatest worry about his crew. There was something more deadly than the sea aboard. In those 12 days of tacking he had lost 50 men dead and had 40 more so seriously ill that they were unable to move below decks in the dark wet hell where no man could stand upright anyway. One of those sun-tanned men among his crew had brought some sort of tropical fever aboard with him. Each day of the gale five more bodies were flung overboard.

For all their struggles against the wind and sea, on January 20th, the *Amsterdam* had still not passed Beachy Head and Klump decided to seek refuge in Pevensey Bay, a well-known spot to shelter from south-west winds.

It was a decision which he could not fail to take. Those of his crew who were not down with the mystery sickness, were completely exhausted. Nothing was dry in their quarters and when each hundred men came off watch every four hours they brought more water with them. Those who shared a hammock were lucky. Those who bedded down beside the 12-pound cannon lay on sodden sacking and had to listen to the ropes which lashed down the guns creaking and protesting at each new lurch of the ship. Some of the sick are said to have drowned when water collected in pools and slopped back and forth in time with the ship's motion.

As Klump fought his ship to shelter through the mountainous seas he might have been forgiven for thinking nothing worse could happen. But it did. Before he was properly in, the ship grounded on a shoal. The next wave lifted her and then dropped her down in the trough so hard that her rudder was ripped away as though made of paper.

She could not now be steered and Klump ordered his anchor

dropped. She drifted a long way before it gripped and she finally swung head to wind off Bexhill.

The anchor seemed firm enough and as a precaution Klump now let go another smaller anchor. Here at least he seemed safe. Once the gale stopped and calm returned he had some hopes that his ship could be repaired enough for him to get round and into Portsmouth Dockyard for proper replacement work to be carried out.

But the gale blew and blew and the *Amsterdam* snubbed and tore at her anchors as the spray billowed up around her. Day after day it went on, though there must have been some sort of lull at one stage as a fishing boat from Hastings came out with offers of help. Whether this offer was genuine or whether the Hastings men were just sizing up a possible wreck, no one can know. There is no written record of what they saw. But certainly nothing could be done until the gale blew itself out.

There the *Amsterdam* might well have stayed until calm returned, but in the early hours of Sunday, January 26th fate struck another blow at Captain Klump. Either the anchor cables could take no more and they parted – or someone cut them.

That someone cut those cables is not unlikely. As far as the crew was concerned nothing could be worse than sitting out at sea and waiting to be struck down by the deadly fever that was still aboard as the growing number of sick below decks openly testified. Nothing could be worse either than looking forward to sailing on after repairs for thousands more sea miles leaving a trail of corpses in her wake. If the ship were beached at least they stood a chance of survival. All the ingredients of a mutiny were there – and it happened.

The crew broke into the ship's cargo of wine and were soon drunk. Some, however, must have kept their heads because the ship's guns were fired repeatedly as a signal of distress. Nothing, of course, could be done to save the ship and the wind drove them steadily towards the shre.

We know exactly what time the guns were fired because letters of the time in the East Sussex Record Office at Lewes tell us that the service at St. Clement's Church was interrupted by the noise at 3 p.m. and, reading between the lines, was abandoned so that the whole congregation could get down to the shore and take their share of the loot.

And looting there undoubtedly was. As most of the town headed for the seashore, the *Amsterdam* came in on the top of the tide until she finally stopped, well and truly beached. Only then did her high stern stop acting like a sail driving her bow on up the shore.

The place she struck is just to the east of the little village of Bulverhythe, almost exactly where William the Conqueror is said to have landed in Britain, and it took some time for the people of Hastings to struggle against the wind the three miles to the actual site.

The first man there was Sir Charles Eversfield. A letter from him describing his disgust that "all the crew were drunk" exists to this day. Very soon a huge crowd had gathered on the beach opposite the stranded ship, but it wasn't until the tide receded that the crew and soldiers, who could still walk, got ashore in safety.

And then the looting began. For a few hours the local people had their chance, then a company of foot soldiers were rushed to the wreck and some sort of order was restored. No one had yet realised that the ship was stuck in a patch of yielding clay.

Three letters of the time in the East Sussex Record office tell very well the story of what happened next. The first is from Mr. George Worge to his father-in-law, John Collier, who was secretary to the Duke of Newcastle. The Duke, as Admiral Of The Sussex Coast, was responsible for all shipwrecks there. Writes Mr. Worge, just two days after the wreck:

"We have had for a long time past the most terrible wheather that I ever remember, and Sunday last in the afternoon a Dutch East Indiaman was drove a shore at Bulverhith, and yesterday I rode down to see her, and from one of her officers who spoke a little English I had this account, that she was called the *Amsterdam*, of that place, and bound for Batavia, about 700 tuns and 52 guns, and had when she came out about two Months agoe three hundred men, abt half of w'ch had been lost by sickness and washed over board, and loaded with money, bale goods and stores of all kinds.

"She was a new ship, and had been all this time beating abt and never got beyond Beachy in her way. She Struck in Pevensy Bay and lost her rudder, and has laid off Bexhill at anchor severall day's. Some of the Hastings people got to her and undertook to carry her to Portsmouth when the wheather would permit, but she could hold out no longer than Sunday.

"She stands in a good place, and in appearance quite whole, and may do so for some months, But no possibility of getting her off. I Believe they will save every thing that is worth saveing, to the great disappointm't of the wreckers who come from all parts of the country for plunder, there was yesterday when I was there more than a thousand of these wretches with long poles and hooks at the Ends.

"But all the soldiers on the coast are there, and behave well at present - they keep the country people off, and their officers keep the soldiers to rights. They have carried to the Custom house at Hastings 27 chests of money, and the other pt of her ladeing will be carried to Hastings as fast as it can be got out. One chest was emptied of its money by somebody, and, it's said, was so before it came out of the ship. But it's gone, and by whome is not known.

"I could get no certain acct of the quantity of money, some said three-score thousand pounds, others made it a great deal more, and others much less. The value of the Ship and cargoe is uncertain, but two hundred thousand pounds was the generall estimate.

"There was three women on board, who are now at Hasting. When I was down there were abt forty sick men in the ship, w'ch they afterwards got out and sent to Hasting. I saw Sir Chs. Eversfield there, who told me he was down when she came on Shore, and that all the crew were drunk, and so were all of them that I saw yesterday".

The *Amsterdam* was sinking into the sand and the looters were not having much success, apart from that one chest of silver. The next letter, to Mr. Collier again from his personal secretary, Richard Patrick, makes this very clear:

"The ship is really a meloncholy sight to behold, for she lyes on shore, upon a boggy sand, that she is swerved almost as high as her Upper Deck, and notwithstanding all the contrivances imagineable, the main hatches can't be open'd, so that it's feared most part of the cargoe in the main hold will perish in the sand.

"They have endeavoured to burn the decks, and have made a bone fire thereupon, which had no effect, notwithstanding they burnt, at one time, two hundred batt faggots.

"They have also endeavoured to blow up the decks with gun powder, but as the ship is so much swerved, she always continues under water, that they can't fix barrels of powder at a proper place for that purpose ..."

The *Amsterdam* continued to "swerve" - a local use of the word meaning to sink - and gradually all dreams of getting at the contents began to fade.

A month after the wreck Mr. Thorpe, the Mayor of Hastings, wrote to Mr. Collier. He had different ideas about the role of the soldiers protecting the wreck:

"The treasure of the ship, amounting to near thirty thousand pounds value, being sent to London has eased us of a Company of Foot, who were the greatest thieves I ever knew, they not only robbed at the ship, but their quarters also. The Dutch soldiers and sailors robed their Officers, as did too many of our own town.

"There was a chest containing fifty Wedges of silver, each weighing about four pounds and a half, broke open the first night, but by one means or another we have recovered thirty six, and a gold watch, but very little of the gold and silver lace and wearing apparel.

"There are some cables and anchors, some provisions, as butter, bacon, beef, and c. saved, also several chest of wine in bottles, of which there is in the ship a great many thousand dozen.

"The ship is so swerved in the sand, that at high water the sea covers her, and at low, her lower Deck is under water. They have endeavoured to blow up her decks with gunpowder, sometimes succeeding, at others not, the powder being obliged to be putt under water, but this morning they blew up a great part of the lower deck, and its thought the composition next the match being too dry, fired so quick, that Mr. Nutt the Engineer perished.

"P.S. the wine is French – if you would have any, please to let me know, I fancy about 1 shilling a bottle will be the price".

For months they tried to salvage the *Amsterdam's* cargo, but finally even the VOC gave up. The Amsterdam sunk deeper and deeper into the sand. In the early 1800's there were one or two attempts to get into the ship, but finally she was abandoned. Over the years the timbers still showed at low Spring tides, but they were just something for holidaymaking children to romp around.

In the end she was forgotten. And would have remained so if it had not been decided to build a sewer outfall some distance offshore and have the landward end just four hundred yards from the wreck site.

William Press and Son Limited were to be the builders and the site agent was Kenneth Young, a local man, who was greatly interested in the history of the area and so knew about the ship. He determined to have a look for her and unlike all those salvors of long ago he really did have the tool to do the job – a mechanical excavator. When the tide let him he dug several deep holes into the wreck position and to his amazement and that of everyone else, up came a slice of eighteenth century life.

In the ooze from the excavator's bucket were a pewter tankard, fine horn combs, a lady's ivory fan, wine-glasses, wine-bottles still full of wine of a kind, brass candlesticks, cartridge cases, leather shoes, bronze smoothing irons, stoneware jugs ... And then the most fantastic find of all – five bronze cannon, still wrapped in the sacking which had covered them when they were stored with the rest of the cargo. Each cannon was dated 1748 and bore the insignia VOC entwined, with a capital A above it for the Amsterdam branch of the Dutch East India Company.

Mr. Young realised the importance of his discovery, reported it, and soon the archaeologists were on the spot. To please them Mr. Young dug another hole beside the ship. To say that the archaeologists were amazed is a great understatement. For there, in a hole in a British beach was a major marine archaeological discovery. Not only was the main mast found to be intact alongside the ship, but six feet down from the upper deck were a row of gun ports, still closed by their lids. It looked as though almost the whole ship was intact from the deck down.

Here buried under the beach was a complete time-capsule of how people lived – and died – aboard an 18th century East Indiaman. Of such importance was it that the site was quickly designated as an historic wreck under the Protection of Wrecks Act 1973. This means that no one, except the archaeologists, can touch her. Even though at low Spring tides today you can stand and see the outline of the *Amsterdam* clearly marked by timbers sticking up from the soggy sand.

News of this discovery was not long in reaching Holland, of course. Now the Dutch Government has claimed ownership and they are working on various schemes to raise her and take her back to Holland for everyone to see in a special museum in Amsterdam. One such scheme being seriously considered is to get the wreck, complete with the five thousand tons of sand which cover her, into a floating caisson and tow her back to Holland. In fact that would mean that Captain Klump's great ship would complete her voyage after a mere 240 years! Captain Klump, by the way, was exonerated of all blame by the Company, made several voyages to the East Indies for them and died in October, 1775 in Holland.

You can still see *Amsterdam* on the beach at Bulverhythe, or at least the shape of her, when the tide is very low. Choose the lowest Spring tide possible.

How to get there

The *Amsterdam*, with her great timbers sticking up from the seabed at low tide, deserves a beautiful walk to the site.

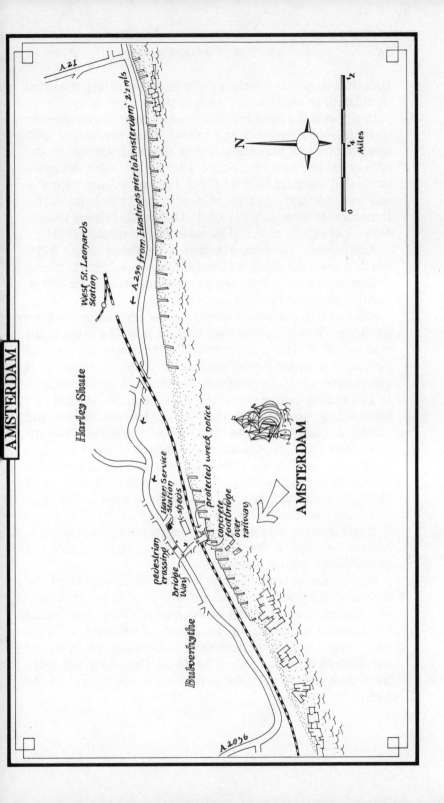

Unfortunately, unless you get there by walking along the beach from Hastings itself, the approach is totally unromantic.

In any case the mark for the site of the wreck is an unlovely concrete footbridge over the railway line, which here runs along the back of the beach. It is on the beachside foot of this railway bridge, next to a notice warning about the danger of swimming when red flags are flying, that you will see the notice that you are within yards of a protected wreck under the Protection of Wrecks Act of 1973. The wreck is almost straight out to sea from the notice. (Ordnance grid reference 778083).

Approach by car from Hastings is by means of the A259, which at first runs along the front and then goes slightly inland. Follow it under a railway bridge then look out for the Haven Service Station on your left.

After a set of pedestrian crossing lights keep a sharp eye out for Bridge Way, a narrow road on your left. The name of the road tells it all. This is the approach to the concrete footbridge. Parking in the road is very restricted with double yellow lines everywhere and evidence of our industrial age well to the fore. In fact the footbridge starts just after a sign at the gates of a yard telling you that this is the Chief Mechanical and Electrical Engineer's Department of St. Leonards. It is the most incongrous approach to any ancient shipwreck that I know. The steps of the footbridge lead you up and over the railway lines and sidings with goods wagons beside great industrial sheds and there at the foot of the steps on the other side is the wreck notice.

If you look out over the beach from the top of the bridge you can see outcrops of the same clay into which the *Amsterdam* sank sticking up quite close to you.

Heaven knows what William the Conqueror would make of the place today because it is here that he is believed to have first landed, just to the east of the hamlet of Bulverhythe. At the approach to the pier in Hastings itself you can see the flat rock which is called the Conqueror's Stone, on which legend says he had his first meal in England. This stone was taken from close to the site of the *Amsterdam* wreck and put by the pier.

In fact the spot has another claim to fame as well. Just to the east of the site is a little place called Bo-Peep. Just offshore you will find on many nautical charts a reef of rocks called Bo-peep Rocks. Bo-Peep? Yes, that's right, the lady with the sheep.

However, according to local legend, that nursery rhyme had nothing to do with such childish things as a shepherdess losing her flock. Let's look at it again:

"Little Bo-Peep has lost her sheep,
And doesn't know where to find them;
Leave them alone and they will come home,
Dragging their tails behind them."

That rhyme, however, loses a lot of its charm when you are told that Bo-Peep refers to the Customs Officers, who are believed to have had a post at Bo-Peep in olden days, and that the sheep are the smugglers, and the tails they dragged behind them were barrels of contraband brandy!

None of this, however, can take away the pleasure of walking out over the sand at really low tides and, skirting the pits dug nearby by lugworm-hunting fishermen, seeing with your own eyes the timbers of that great Dutch East Indiaman poking up from the sand.

CHAPTER FOUR

Mary Rose

The date: July 19, 1545.
The weather: good. Winds light, offshore.

Henry VIII was about to see the flower of his navy, the *Mary Rose*, sink before his eyes with the loss of nearly 700 men, as she sailed out to meet the French in the Solent.

The *Mary Rose* was launched in 1509 as part of Henry VIII's programme of naval rearmament. She was the first ship – or one of the first ships – ever to be fitted with guns below deck and able to fire broadsides through gun ports in her hull. She was a highly successful ship of 600 tons and was about 150 feet long with a beam of 50 feet. In 1513, Sir Edward Howard, who had used her as his flagship in campaigns against the French, wrote to the King describing the *Mary Rose* as "your good ship, the flower I trow of all ships that ever sailed". A high recommendation indeed.

In her in those days were 120 sailors, 251 soldiers (because most naval battles still consisted of grappling and letting the soldiers fight it out), 20 gunners, two pilots, five trumpeters and 36 servants.

However in 1536, the *Mary Rose* was put in for a refit. In fact she was almost rebuilt. She was uprated to 700 tons and her armament increased to 91 guns. With the extra gunners her crew now consisted of some 415 men.

In 1545 England was under threat of invasion by the French, and Henry VIII went to Portsmouth Harbour to review his fleet. Amongst over 100 ships gathered there was *Mary Rose*. In fact, by the time King Henry reached Portsmouth, beacons were burning to warn that the French fleet was out in the Channel and orders had gone to all the King's ships to join the Fleet at Portsmouth.

Shortly after his arrival in Portsmouth, Henry appointed Sir George Carewe to be his vice-Admiral aboard *Mary Rose*. Sir George was one of the King's particular favourites. Captain of the *Mary Rose* was Roger Grenville, another very experienced seaman, which makes what was to follow even more surprising.

While the King was dining with his Lord Admiral John Dudley, Viscount Lisle, aboard the flagship *Greate Henry*, the French were sighted with 235 ships off the north-east corner of the Isle of Wight. The meal, it would seem, broke up rather hastily. The English tactics were either to try and lure the French into the shallows of the Hamilton Bank just outside the harbour entrance, or to shepherd them into the deep water channel which would bring them under the fire of the great guns of the newly-completed Southsea Castle, one of Henry VIII's defence system of coastal forts.

The light winds made either plan very difficult and it was the French who made the first move. Four of their oared galleys moved in to exchange shots with the English Fleet.

For what happened immediately after that meal on the flagship we can go to the report of Sir Peter Carewe, who was the younger brother of Sir George, the King's vice-admiral. This is how he told it:

"And first he hath secret talks with the Lord Admiral, and then he hath the like with Sir George Carewe, and at his departure from him, took his chain from his neck, with a great wistle of gold pendant to the same, and did put it about the neck of the said Sir George Carewe, giving him also therewith many good and comfortable words.

"The King then took his boat, and rowed to the land, and every other captain went to his ship appointed unto him. Sir George Carewe being entered into his ship commanded every man to take his place, and the sails to be hoysted; but the same was no sooner done, but that the *Mary Rose* began to heel, that is, to lean on the one side.

"Sir Gawen Carewe (the Carewes' uncle) being then in his own ship, and seeing the same called for the master of his ship and told him thereof, and asked him what it meant, who answered, that if she did heel, she was like to be cast away. Then the said Sir Gawen, passing by the *Mary Rose*, called out to Sir George Carewe, asking him how he did? who answered, that he had a sort of knaves, whom he could not rule.

"And it was not long after, but that the said *Mary Rose*, thus heeling more and more, was drowned, with 700 men which were in her; whereof very few escaped. It chanced unto this gentleman, as the common proverb is 'the more cooks, the worst potage'. He had in his ship a hundred mariners, the worst of them being able to be a master in the best ship within the realm, and these so maligned and disdained one the other, that refusing to do that which they should do, were careless to that they ought to do; and so contending in envy, perished in frowardness.

"The King this meanwhile stood on the land, and saw this tragedy, as also the lady the wife to Sir George Carewe, who with that sight fell into a swooning. The King being oppressed with sorrow of every side, comforted her, and thanked God for the other, hoping that of a hard beginning there would follow a better ending. And notwithstanding this loss, the service appointed went forward, as soon as wind and weather would serve; and the residue of the fleet, being about the number of one hundred and five sails, took the seas.

"The Frenchmen perceiving the same, like as a sort of sheep running into the fold, they shifted away, and got them into their harbours; thinking it better to lie there in a safe skin, than to encounter with them of whom they should little win."

The French of course did not see it like that. In fact a historian of the time, du Bellay, wrote: "Fortune favoured our fleet, in this manner, for above an hour, during which time, among other damages which the English received, the *Mary Rose* one of their principal ships, was sunk by our cannon, and of the five or six hundred men which were on board, only five and thirty escaped."

Who was right? Certainly if Sir Peter was right and the *Mary Rose* was carrying 700 men, she had nearly 300 more than her normal complement and when she heeled their weight would have forced the gun ports underwater and let the sea rush in.

If she had been sunk by French cannonfire surely Henry VIII, watching, resplendent in cloth of gold, would hardly have accepted it as an accidental loss which all English contemporary reports confirm?

We may know the answer very soon. In fact the answer may be known by the time you read this book. The *Mary Rose*, after having been located by British Sub-Aqua Club amateur divers led by Mr. Alexander McKee in 1967, has been dived on extensively since. Hundreds of amateur divers of the Club have given up their holidays to work underwater on the wreck just off Southsea Castle under the direction of archaeologists headed by Mrs. Margaret Rule. As I write we know that the vast proportion of the wreck is intact after being slowly uncovered by divers from the clinging Solent mud. Hundreds of priceless objects of Tudor times have been recovered from her holds and the ancient ship is being prepared for lifting and placing for all to see in a special Tudor ship museum at Eastney, Portsmouth.

Visiting the museum can hardly be described as a walk to a wreck site – or can it? – but no book of wreck sites on the coasts of Southern England would be complete without the story of the *Mary Rose*.

CHAPTER FIVE

Assurance and Campen

The date: April 24th, 1753.
The weather: fine with clear skies, perfect visibility, and a light westerly wind.

A proud boast was about to lose the Royal Navy one of its best 44-gun ships – and send the man responsible into the prison they called "Hell upon Earth".

His Excellency Governor Trelawney was the man who prompted the boast. David Patterson, the sailing master of *H.M.S. Assurance*, the man who made it in the early hours of that fine April day.

To know how and why it happened and how and why that Navy fifth-rate was wrecked, we need to go back a little in time. Governor Trelawney and his lady were coming home from Jamaica, where he had acquitted himself well. Now after a voyage that had been blessed with fair weather all the way, he was within sight of England, in fact the white cliffs of the Needles were clear on the starboard bow as they started to enter the Needles Channel.

Governor Trelawney had served his country well in Jamaica, but he hadn't forgotten to serve himself as well. Among his baggage were a number of small bags, which would have chinked if they hadn't been packed together so tightly. Those pieces-of-eight were the result of careful, and in the Governor's opinion fair, administration and allocation of contracts. Those bags were going to see him through many an English

winter, which he knew would be in sharp contrast to the balmy days of his stay in Jamaica.

So the Governor considered himself fortunate, not only in the pleasant voyage, but also in the Captain and crew, and the ship which had brought him home.

Assurance ran on steadily. She too was coming home for she had been built at the Heather Yard at Bursledon and since she had been launched on September 29th, 1747, she had spent a deal of her sea time in the West Indies.

Captain Carr Scrope was enjoying seeing the thin line of white turn into the cliffs of the Isle of Wight. For he was coming home too, but his pleasure was greatly enhanced by the thought that his career in the Navy had taken a distinct turn for the better. He had enjoyed his days in Jamaica. But he had only been commanding a sloop when his promotion to captain had come through on November 14th, 1752, and he had been given command of *Assurance* for her homeward voyage. Standing on her deck watching the light spread, he knew that though he had no bags of silver below decks like the Governor, at least his promotion had meant that all was forgiven. For to be honest, Scrope's Naval career, up to that time, had not gone well. The real trouble had started after his appointment as lieutenant aboard the *Neptune* in 1742. The *Neptune* had sailed to join the Mediterranean Fleet and young Lieutenant Scrope had found himself in February 1744 off Toulon with the fleet of over 20 ships under the command of Admiral Mathews.

England and Spain had been at war since 1739, but England and France, though undoubtedly on opposite sides, had not yet actually declared war. It was all very confusing. Spain was sending troops to Northern Italy to attack Austria's Italian possessions and France was helping Spain to do so by placing the port of Toulon at the Spaniards' disposal. The French also seemed willing to provide ships to help the Spaniards convey the troops to Italy.

So Admiral Mathews had a problem. But he decided that he would be justified in attacking the French ships if they formed a joint fleet with the Spaniards and sailed together out of Toulon. So he kept his fleet just off the port and waited.

On February 9th, the joint fleet came out of harbour all right, but there was no sign of the troops' transports. This set the Admiral a real teaser. If he attacked the Franco-Spanish fleet, the transports would be able to slip out and away. But if he stayed and waited for the transports he would lose his chance of engaging the enemy fleet. Unfortunately, he tried to do both. His plan was to engage the fleet, then double back and take the transports. It sounded excellent, but the trouble was that the rigid rules of sea fighting as laid down by the Admiralty didn't allow for such quick tactics. According to the book, Mathews should have first of all ensured that he held the windward position. He did. So that was all right.

But the next rule of fighting, Admirals for the use of, said that before he bore down on the enemy, he should so arrange his line of ships that each ship was opposed to the correspond-ing ship in the enemy's line. Now Mathews couldn't wait until this was exactly so and signalled the attack as soon as he could. As a result, with everyone else going by the book, a mighty muddle ensued and Mathews had to break off the battle very quickly.

Courts-martial galore followed this fiasco and Mathews was dismissed the Service. This was grossly unfair because he had fought hard, but he had broken the rules so he had to go.

And in the middle of all the courts-martial was young Lieutenant Scrope, who was called as a witness at the trials of captains, vice-admirals and even Admiral Mathews himself. Not the sort of role to win friends and influence people. But Scrope was only a witness and the Navy promoted him to commander on August 11th, 1746 and gave him the *White-haven*. She was very small and was only described as an "armed ship". Scrope didn't command her for very long because in September one year later, she caught fire and sank off the coast of Ireland. Seventeen were lost, but the rest took to the boats and were saved.

Once again Scrope found himself at a court-martial, but this time it was his own. Much to his relief, he was acquitted of the charge of having lost his ship through neglect, but things were obviously not going well for him.

When he was given a small sloop to command and packed off to the Jamaica station, Scrope feared that his chances of promotion had come to an abrupt end. His promotion to captain and command of the *Assurance* had, however, cleared such nasty thoughts from his mind.

So Scrope, in that dawn of April 24th, 1753, was content. He had had nothing but fair winds from Jamaica, and even good weather up the Channel after their brief stop at Lisbon. The crew, like most home-coming crews, had behaved well; so had his officers. In particular, Scrope had been pleased with his master, David Patterson, who seemed sober, was certainly diligent, and had the right appreciation of his position. The captain commanded the ship. The sailing master sailed it where the captain ordered. But the captain could overrule the master at any time he felt necessary. Patterson completely accepted that, unlike some masters Scrope could name, who gave the impression that they were much more important than the captain.

With the Isle of Wight coming closer and closer every moment, Captain Scrope felt quite happy to leave the decision about their course to David Patterson. If they went through the Needles Channel they would avoid the long haul around the Island to their destination at Spithead. But Scrope gave the decision to Patterson.

"Will you take her through?" Patterson nodded. But Scrope wanted to make sure that his question was understood – "She's in your charge then?". "She is", said Patterson clearly.

The light westerly wind was ideal. Later Patterson was to say that the wind was west-by-north or west-north-west, but it made no difference to his decision to take her through the narrows.

David Patterson carefully followed the sailing directions on his charts, noted that he had Alum Bay open with Needle Rock. A glance at the compass – north-east-a-half-east. Then a look aloft. He noted: "All sails out, but the studding sails, and the shore tack at the cathead". The sails filled more fully and *Assurance* moved gracefully ahead.

But for all his confidence, David Patterson had never taken

any ship through that channel before. True, he had been part of the crew of many ships that had passed through, but he had never been in command of one himself. Perhaps he worried about that first time, but if he did he didn't show it. It was then that Governor Trelawney put the question: "How close to the Needles will we go?" Patterson replied with the boast that was to cost him dear. "We will pass so close that the fly of the ensign might actually touch the rock!"

What the Governor said to that is not recorded, but the truth about Patterson's boast is that he was probably more afraid of the Shingles on the port side. These great sandbanks appeared to Patterson to be unusually high out of the water. He feared too that they might have shifted their charted position. Not such a ridiculous fear either, for any Isle of Wight sailor will tell you that the sands do shift this way and that.

So Patterson set his course closer to the Needles than he should have done and relied on the tide "horsing" the ship to the west. They were now almost up to the Needles and the 133-foot long ship was going well. The Needles came very close and it looked as though the master's boast would come true. Suddenly the leadsman shouted: "A quarter less five".

Only then did Patterson have some inkling of his danger. "Cast again - quick", he shouted. But, before the lead line even left the man's hand, the ship struck with a grinding crash which stopped her as though she had run head-on into a stone quay.

The dismay that raced through Patterson's brain was only matched by the utter disbelief. There was no rock charted where he had struck - in fact the charts showed nothing but deep water. A year and a half he had been master of the *Assurance* and now it looked as though he had lost not only the ship but all his future.

Within an hour the water was coming in faster than the pumps could throw it out. Scrope knew that the ship was lost and soon he would face yet another court-martial. But now he tried everything to save what could be saved from the disaster. In fact there was plenty of time. Governor Trelawney supervised the loading of his fortune into one of the boats, though one of the little bags was lost in the flooded hold. And several hours later, the *Assurance* slid off the rock and into deeper water.

The Admiralty didn't waste time about their enquiries into the cause of the wreck. By an Admiralty Order dated May 1st, 1753, "The Honorable Edward Boscawen, Rear-Admiral of the White Squadron of His Majesty's Fleet and Commander in Chief of His Majesty's ships at Portsmouth Harbour" was directed to "Assemble a court-martial for enquiring into the cause of the loss of His Majesty's late ship the *Assurance* the 24th April last, when, endeavouring to go through the Needles, the said ship struck in the Narrows and was lost, and into the Conduct of the Officers and Men on that Occasion".

Boscawen didn't waste time either. The court-martial took place on board *H.M.S. Tyger* in Portsmouth Harbour on May 11th, 1753 with Boscawen as President. The other judges were Captains Robert Petty, Jonathan Montagu, George Bridges Rodney, the Hon. Sam Barrington, Roger Martin, Charles Catford, Julian Legg and Sam Marshall.

It was an intimidating array of Naval power, but not one which would indulge in the sort of politicking that Scrope had seen years before at the court-martial of Admiral Mathews. Admiral Boscawen, for example, was a stern man, but whose reputation for fair dealing was a legend among the crews of the ships he had commanded. He was an odd mixture of sea-dog and scholar, who would write letters to his wife which contained such poetic phrases as "To be sure I lose the fruits of the land, but then I am gathering the flowers of the sea". Scrope knew that whatever the result, Boscawen would see to it that it was properly arrived at and all the evidence duly considered.

Boscawen was the first to speak: "Captain Scrope, have you any complaint to make against any of your officers or company for neglect of duty, disobedience to command, or being in anyway instrumental or contributing towards the loss of the *Assurance*?"

"No, sir", replied Scrope, "they all did their duty and behaved as they ought."

"Then how came the ship to be lost?"

"I imagine it must be by the course in which the master was mistaken." It was a true, but damning statement and Boscawen did not let it pass. "Did the master willingly take charge of the ship, or was it forced upon him?"

"He undertook it willingly", replied Scrope.

Boscawen then called David Patterson. "Master, you hear what the captain says as to your willingly taking charge of the ship?"

"I did, sir."

"How had you the wind?"

"West by north or west-north-west."

"And how came you then to lose the ship?"

"I can but ill account for it. I thought we were in a fair way, having Alum Bay open with the Needle Rock. When the man at the lead called out just before the ship struck 'a quarter less five', I called to the man to heave another cast quick ... before he could do so, the ship struck."

"Do you remember what course you steered?"

"North-east-a-half-east by the compass."

"What sail had you aboard?"

"All out but studding sails."

The questions were drummed out one after the other, but Patterson kept his head.

"Did the ship go ashore with all sails full?"

"Yes, sir."

"Had you ever charge of a ship through the Needles before?"

"No. I have been in and out often, but never had charge of a ship."

"How came you to keep so near the Needle Rock where the Channel is so wide and you had the wind so large?"

"At the latter end of the ebb, I was afraid of the Shingles which the tide set us directly upon. They appeared so high out of the water I concluded they had shifted nearer the Island as they will do sometimes."

The question of his boast was raised and to Patterson's relief the assembled captains took, or seemed to take, little notice of it. Boscawen was soon on to what he considered a vital point.

"As you was abreast of the Needles and the wind large why did you not go ... why did you not go round the Island?"

The implication was clear – had Patterson hazarded the ship just to save a little time? There was only one answer he could give. "I thought we should come sooner to Spithead." There was a long silence during which the only sound was that of the clerk's quill scratching frantically to keep up.

Boscawen changed tack again. "Did you know there was a rock so near the Needles as that you struck upon?"

"I did not know anything of a rock so far off and few people did."

"Would you have any of the officers called in your justification?"

Patterson declined. In truth, he could not see that they could do anything, but give him a good character and it was not that which was being attacked. He did, however, ask for three pilots who knew the area well to be examined. So they were called and as might be expected all gave evidence that they, too, had no idea of any rock in the place where the *Assurance* struck.

Which today seems strange because aerial pictures show the rock clearly. And even though aeroplanes were not available in those days, any ship going close to the Needles must have been able to see the dark shape of the rock through the water at low tide. But then, perhaps, no one went that close on an ebbing tide. Certainly not as close as Patterson had gone.

After further evidence, which added nothing except to prove that David Patterson was "a sober, careful, diligent officer", the court was adjourned for the Captains to consider their verdict. On their return, Boscawen turned to his fellow judges and put the vital questions:

"Is it your opinion that Captain Scrope was at all accessory to the loss of the *Assurance?*" "No", said the Captains.

"Is it your opinion that the lieutenants were at all accessory to the loss of the said ship?" "No", said the Captains.

"Is it your opinion that the rest of the officers and crew were at all accessory?" "No", said the Captains.

"Is it your opinion that the loss of the ship was owing to the unskilfulness, negligence or carelessness of the master?"

"No", said the Captains – and if David Patterson heaved a sigh of relief he was much too premature, because the Captains had not finished and finally sorted out a form of words that the clerk could pen ... "But we attribute it to his ignorance of the rock the ship run upon, which is generally said to be little known". So the Captains had not been totally convinced by the evidence of the pilots.

"What article does the master fall under?" Boscawen prompted them. "Under part of the 26th Article by running the ship unskilfully upon the rock."

"What punishment do you award him?"

"In regard to the general good character of the master, the court are unanimously of opinion that he be imprisoned three months in the Marshalsea."

Poor David Patterson. The prison to which he had been condemned was a diabolical place to spend even a day let alone three months. It stood opposite Maypole Alley, in Borough High Street, Southwark, London. It was the county jail for felons, the Admiralty jail for pirates and masters who lost ships on rocks, and a debtors prison too.

It was crowded, it was filthy and it stank. Disease ended many a sentence before it had fully run. In fact in the same year that David Patterson was committed there, John Wesley described it as "a picture of Hell upon Earth". It was the prison made infamous by Charles Dickens in "Little Dorrit" and it had been a prison since the fourteenth century with little if any improvement since then.

We know nothing more of what happened then to David Patterson. One can only hope that he survived and finally got back to sea, but no records seem to mention him again. Captain Scrope, however, seemed none the worse for the court-martial. He got another ship, commanded H.M.S. Dolphin in April, 1756, and served with great gallantry during the siege of Minorca. In 1761 he died while commanding H.M.S. Hampton Court.

Goose Rock, for that is the name today of the one that the Assurance struck, has since claimed other victims. In 1811,

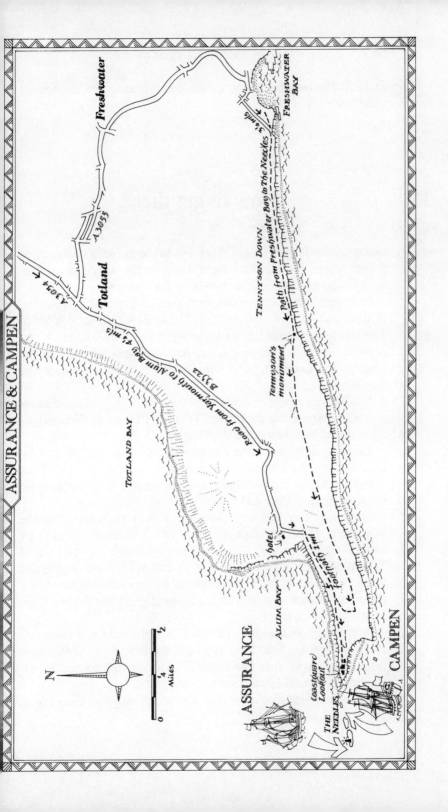

H.M.S. Pomone, a fifth-rate, sank there, and so did a schooner called *Dream* in 1837.

How to get there

Once on the Isle of Wight there are two approaches to vantage points where you can look right down on the wreck, for divers have found that she is still there with her cannon.

First approach is from the ferry port of Yarmouth. Take the A3054 and at the junction in Totland with the A3055 to Freshwater on your left carry straight on until you reach the hotel at Alum Bay. Here you can park and walk up towards the Coastguard Lookout, from which you can look out over the Needles.

Second approach and a much longer walk is from Freshwater Bay along the cliffs over Tennyson Down to Tennyson's Monument and then on to the Needles.

Looking down on a fine day or a stormy one, no matter what the weather, the Needles are an impressive sight. Goose Rock is slightly to the right of Needle Rock on which the lighthouse sits (See picture Page 46).

On a fine day you may well see a boat anchored over the rock with divers at work. For the wreck is being studied by archaeological divers, led by Derek Williams of the Isle of Wight, who discovered *Assurance's* last resting place. He did years of research work and then on his very first dive on the place he thought she should be, he landed on the seabed right on top of her cannon!

Assurance's wreckage is mingled with that of the *Dream* and *H.M.S. Pomone*. Searching among the remains Derek Williams discovered proof that Governor Trelawney did not get all his savings off her. He found some of the coins.

But when you look down on this wreck site you are looking

out over another, which can truly be called a treasure ship. Only 500 yards away from Goose Rock, on the left hand side of the Needles as you look down on them, in the gap between the nearest jagged white peaks lies a Dutch East Indiaman.

Here too you may well see a diving boat, for another team are surveying the underwater remains of the *Campen*, sunk on October 14th, 1627. They have already recovered over 3,000 silver coins from the wreck, which they found by accident on a pleasure dive!

How did the *Campen* get there? By disobeying orders, that's how. Before she sailed from Holland with the rest of the autumn fleet, laden with silver to exchange for pepper and spices in the East Indies, her orders from the Dutch East India Company were quite clear – "under no circumstances to anchor on English Ground". This was because James I, in retaliation for attacks on English ships on similar trade missions, harassed Dutch ships whenever he could catch them in British waters.

Orders given in the quiet of some port are one thing. Those same orders are not the same when you are being driven by a howling south-westerly gale. That is what happened to the Dutch fleet of which *Campen* was a part. Two captains obviously thought that those orders were worth disobeying if they could get to shelter behind the Isle of Wight.

Those two ships, the *Flying Dragon* and the *Campen*, must have been in dire straits in that storm – for they tried to get to shelter by going between the jagged rocks of the Needles. Only someone driven quite crazy with fear would have attempted to take a ship through that narrow gap, filled as it was with spray from the huge seas which pounded on the Needles. The *Flying Dragon* hit bottom but managed to surf through on the back of a giant wave and then ran aground in the Solent, damaged, but safer than she had been. Next to try was the *Campen*. She didn't make it, striking the middle Needle and being smashed to pieces by the walls of water which also stormed through the gap.

A great deal of salvage was done at the time and thousands of silver coins were raised as well as her guns and anchors and anything else that could be grabbed or dragged up. So it was amazing that today's divers found more coins and a pile of over one hundred huge lead ingots in only 30 feet of water. A survey of the wreck site is now being carried out and artifacts discovered will eventually go on display at the Rijksmuseum in Amsterdam.

Another more exciting viewing point for the Needles comes by visiting the old Needles Batteries, which are being restored by the National Trust. The entrance is clearly marked "Needles Old Battery 1862". Go through the tunnel into the parade ground, which is where the guns were. These heavy guns were installed to beat off any threat to Britain from the new French ironclads. By 1900 these guns were backed by searchlights to pick out any such warship and hold it while the guns got the range. They were never fired in anger.

In 1913, one of the very first anti-aircraft guns was mounted in the parade ground where you now stand. A one-pound pom-pom, it too was never fired in anger. Other guns mounted in the same place did however have their moments. In particular guns of the battery fired at two German E-boats in 1943, but apparently caused no damage.

From the parade ground walk towards the Coastguard House which is slightly to the left ahead of you. When you reach the foot of a guy-rope to the Coastguard mast, you will see a square block built of bricks. This is the entrance to a tunnel. A time-switch light is not always functioning so it is a good idea to take a torch with you.

First you go down a circular iron staircase and then 200 feet along a tunnel with a gently sloping gradient. Suddenly you will emerge on to the 1899 searchlight position, which has the most splendid view of the Needles and our wreck sites. Once again it is the National Trust who have restored the way to this point and it is well-worth braving the tunnel for the view.

CHAPTER SIX

Herzogin Cecilie

The date: July 18th, 1936.
The weather: a south-easterly gale, low cloud.

The sea built up until a swine of a swell surged into Starehole Bay, near Salcombe, South Devon, and the long fight to save one of the last of the great clipper sailing ships was over.

They called her *The Duchess* and duchess she was as she creamed across the world's oceans with all her huge sails set at her top speed of over 20 knots. But her real name was the *Herzogin Cecilie*.

The *Herzogin Cecilie* took the nickname of the *Duchess*, not from her speed which was not quite a world record – the Yankee clipper *James Baines* held that with 21 knots notched up for one hour's sailing in 1856 – but from her figurehead, which was of the Duchess Cecilie, daughter of the Duke of Oldenburg.

This great ship started her life in the Rickmers yards at Bremerhaven in Germany where she was launched in April, 1902. A 3,111-ton steel four-master, this tall ship was to have almost exactly 34 years of life before she died in Starehole Bay near the mouth of the Salcombe Estuary.

But if her sailing life was not long, it was certainly exciting. At first she was the crack cadet-training ship of the Norddeutscher Lloyd, but at the outbreak of World War One, she was voluntarily interned in Chile where the start of hostilities had caught her. At the end of the war she was handed over by the Germans to the French as part of the reparations. All German efforts to repurchase her were refused and the French finally sold her to a Finnish shipping firm.

It was then that she really showed what she could do. During the grain races to Australia she left most of her rivals standing. Which is not surprising when you know that with all sails spread she had an acre of canvas up to trap the wind. With that driving power, her 336ft-long hull, which was only 46 feet wide, smashed its way from Australia to England in under 90 days. In one day she sailed over 341 nautical miles; in seven she put 1,180 miles behind her keel. In fact on one run from Melbourne, Australia to Taltal, Chile, she managed 2,120 nautical miles in seven days – a record which has never been equalled by any other sailing ship.

Fortunately, although the *Herzogin Cecilie* will never sail again, we do know what it was like on board her at full speed because her mate Elis Karlsson wrote about his life in this tall ship and tells us what it was like when a gale hit her:

"The hands had barely finished their tasks when it hit us. The deep tone in the rigging rose suddenly to a brutal howl and the deck under my feet gave a jerk as if the ship had stumbled; then she leapt ahead. The day was swept away and twilight descended with the hail-filled wind, and the surface of the sea was beaten into smoky spume. The smaller, irregular wave formations were flattened or torn to shreds; the big West-wind rollers, too mighty to be flattened even by such a wind, rose steeper at their crests and hurried their pace.

"For some moments the ship kept up with the seas. On the wind-flattened ridge, with surging white water up to her rails as if in a huge foam-bath, she stormed along with a crumbling avalanche of breaking crest under her, her jib-boom pointing into the valley below and ahead.

"Slowly she lost the race as the undertow made itself felt, and her bows were lifted by the shoulder of the sea; for a while she lingered on the windward slope, her jib-boom thrusting at the screaming murk; slowly she sank down into the comparative quiet of the valley, which echoed with the turmoil above,

6   *Herzogin Cecilie* aground in Starehole Bay

where the hail-mixed spindrift beat a frenzied tattoo on the straining canvas ...

"Something must carry away, nothing can withstand this, I thought. In my mind I was feverishly busy checking up on the gear, although I knew full well that nothing could be done. When had I renewed that wire, when had I turned that sheet-chain? Would that sheet-block sheave be strong enough?

"Every now and then I glanced at the helmsmen and eventually it dawned on me that they hardly moved the wheels. And yet the ship was definitely on course, dead before the wind. She had no time to roll in her headlong rush to Eastward and she was sailing herself!

"I was watching spell-bound the most awe-inspiring, and at the same time the most magnificent sight I shall ever see. I knew then that nothing would carry away; nothing would stop this marvellous ship in this her hour; she was part of the elements; as she was carried eastward in the heart of the gale, ship and the elements were one.

"The spectacle was so overwhelming in its display of power that ordinary awareness, stark fear, or even apprehension vanished and were replaced by an exultant feeling of oneness with the elements and the ship. I knew then that all was well and stood there revelling in it all, a spectator yet a part of it".

That happened on the *Duchess's* last voyage. It was to be her fastest-ever run home from Australia to Falmouth, in 86 days. In Falmouth she was given orders to sail to Ipswich and on April 24th, at eight in the evening, she set out once again. The night was dark with rain and the wind was a moderate south-westerly. But they had only four hours of this good wind, before it dropped and the rain became fog.

It is said that her captain, Sven Eriksson had dreamed of his ship going on the rocks in fog and that up to the last minute Mrs. Eriksson tried to persuade him not to sail from Falmouth, so strongly did she believe in his dream, but certainly the *Duchess* did not heave-to, and continued to feel her way forward through the light swell with her manual fog-horn being sounded every two minutes.

At 3 a.m. the night broke, but the fog remained. Suddenly Captain Eriksson became aware of a dark shape through the fog. He had no doubts - "Hard over to starboard", he yelled. But it was too late. The deck jumped sharply under the crew's feet. They were aground.

Elis Karlsson recorded it like this:

"The ship lifted then struck again with a sickening jar; then the swell lifted her again and she drifted away from the hump of rock ahead and, broadside on, current or swell carried her towards a steep cliff on our port side. The Captain ordered me to let go both anchors; the ship took ground perhaps a cablelength from the cliff ...

"She was making water quickly in the fore-hold but comparatively little in the after-hold. As I went aft to report, Larsen, one of our Danes, approached me and asked if he ought to swim ashore with a message. I brought him along to the Captain. After he had assured us that he was a strong swimmer, the captain gave his permission for Larsen to make the attempt.

"Tensely we watched the young Dane swimming away from the ship with powerful strokes, until he disappeared amongst the heaving swell and swirling fog. How was he to get through the swell creaming white through the mist at the foot of the cliff? I asked myself. Was he to sacrifice himself for us all to no purpose?

"Then we saw him coming back; his strokes were slower, but he still beat the current and the swell. I was well pleased when he stood on deck again, exhausted but unhurt. Larsen had discovered that there was no way off that sheer cliff. The captain gave orders for the crew to collect their belongings, and the Second and I saw to it that the boats were ready. While we were checking the boats we heard a hail from the fog on our port side; the Salcombe lifeboat had arrived.

"We learned from the crew of the lifeboat that the high cliff on our port side was Bolt Head, and that we had struck the Hamstone, a few cablelengths off the shore. The coxwain of the Salcombe lifeboat, Tom Distin, told me that about a hundred yards astern of us lay the bones of the clipper *Halloween*; she ran ashore there in 1887".

The lifeboat stood by for three hours. By then the forward well-deck was awash and the Captain ordered 22 of the crew to be taken off. This left the Captain, his wife, the two mates and four seamen aboard. In the afternoon the rocket apparatus crew got a line aboard and communication with the shore was established. Then they started work getting personal gear ashore by means of the breeches buoy rigged from the top of the cliffs, which were now lined with a solid mass of watchers in both directions as far as the men on the stricken ship could see.

Of course, it wasn't long before the big French and German tugs were on the scene – they almost scented work. The French tugs were the well-known *Abeille No. 16* and *Abeille No. 24*, close behind them came the German *Seefalke*, veteran of many a hazardous tow. But none of the tugs would take the task on. They all thought there was no chance left for the *Duchess*.

On board though, they had not given up hope. The main task was to lighten ship and night and day the work went on.

Ashore went sails and rope. Down came the top-gallant and royal yards and off they went to Salcombe. Small coasters started shifting as much of the wheat cargo as they could. Some 450 tons were salved undamaged. The rest was fit only for pig food. But the weather stayed fine.

The battle to save the *Duchess* was the talk of the country thanks to daily reports in all the newspapers. A fund was started and a donation of £500 came all the way from Canada. Suddenly it looked as though the tall ship could be saved. Pumps were installed on the deck and now the tugs would try to move her.

The plan was to tow the *Herzogin Cecilie* into Salcombe, the rest of the cargo would then be removed, the holes in her hull temporarily patched, and finally she would be towed to dry dock in Plymouth for full and proper repairs.

But the local council, reflecting local feelings, refused to allow her to be towed right into Salcombe fearing that the stench of the rotting wheat – she had after all been on the rocks for seven long weeks – would bring disease, or at least would do nothing for the holiday trade.

The *Duchess* was finally pulled off the rocks by the Hamstone on June 19th and brought round to the sheltered cove of Starehole Bay. Not that this was an easy job. With the pumps and crews from Plymouth Dockyard working flat out, with two tugs pulling and a Spring tide helping, they finally got her up off her rocky couch and into Starehole Bay where she was allowed to settle gently on to a sandy bed.

Unfortunately no one knew at the time just how thin that sandy mattress was. Underneath lay a rocky base. But they didn't know and a rope-bridge was rigged from the ship to shore and a gang of volunteers, largely composed of Cambridge University students on vacation, started getting the rest of the wet wheat, now swollen into a solid mass, out of her. They did well, reducing the original 4,250 tons down to nearly 1,000. But as they worked so did the ship.

She worked herself down through nearly 12 feet of sand on to a ridge of solid rock. She had just about reached the rock when the weather broke. On July 18th, a south-easterly gale sent a great swell surging into Starehole Bay. Elis Karlsson knew she was finished. Waves washed away the rope bridge to shore ... "We stood listening to rivets snapping with reports like pistol-shots; the ship was working heavily in the swell and had reached rock. Staunchions between the decks bent and buckled. It was the end".

Now was the time to strip the wreck of what was left. Her figurehead went to the maritime Museum at Alands, home of the great sailing ships, in Finland, and the wreck was sold to a Kingsbridge metal dealer, Messrs. Noyce, for £225.

But it wasn't really the end of the *Duchess*. She stayed upright, masts still standing proud for a long time. Holiday-makers gazed down on her from the cliff walk and braver spirits swam out to her. But though the sea hadn't finished the job, it came back to do so almost exactly eleven months after her wrecking. This storm broke her up. Her masts crashed down and overnight she was gone from sight except for a dark shape under the water. And that water is not very deep for at its deepest the wreck is only 24 feet under and at low water spring tides what is left of the bow will still sometimes break the surface.

How to get there

Approach is from Salcombe. Drive through the town, keeping the estuary on your left, until you come to either North Sands beach car park or alternatively park further on at South Sands. Be warned, the parking at South Sands fills up very early in the day during the holiday season. South Sands is the nearest approach. After parking, follow the signposts for the Youth Hostel, Sharpitor, or the National Trust sign for the coast path to Bolt Head.

You will soon reach Sharpitor with its gardens of tropical

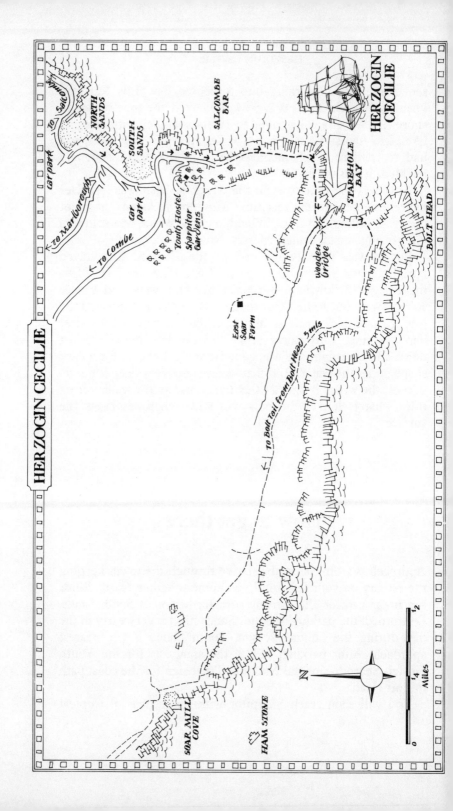

plants and palms, which are open to the public. There too is the Youth Hostel. The museum there has some relics from the *Herzogin Cecilie* - even the heads of pitchforks, used in attempts to move the cargo, which were found by divers on the wreck.

Now follow the sign for the Courtenay Walk and Bolt Tail. Soon the well-paved walk begins to ascend through trees and you are walking along the cliffs overlooking the deadly Salcombe Bar at the entrance to the Estuary. This Bar is in fact a sandbank over which the water is very shallow, and at certain states of wind and tide the sea boils.

In fact so violent does the sea become that on October 27th, 1916, the Salcombe lifeboat, the *William and Emma,* was capsized by huge waves and of the 15-man crew only two survived. The lifeboat had gone out in a south-westerly gale to the aid of a schooner, whose crew, while the lifeboat was on the way, were rescued from the shore by rocket line and breeches-buoy. When the lifeboat returned and prepared to cross the Bar a huge wave hit the stern, tossing the boat high in the air and broadside to the waves. Another wave immediately capsized her, drowning all but two of the crew.

The Bar is said to have been the inspiration for Tennyson's "Crossing the Bar". Certainly the views which are clear once you have left the trees are inspiring. Go through a kissing-gate and there are seats on which you can sit and watch the boat traffic of Salcombe.

Towering above you are the Pinnacles, wind-shaped fingers of rock, and now some steps lead to another viewing place. Then the path drops towards Starehole Bay and the wreck of the *Duchess.* If you want to, you can take a left-hand path down to the cove itself, but so that you can look down and see the remains of the wreck through the usually clear water, it is better to stay on the upper path, following the sign for Bolt Head.

When you are over the centre of Starehole Bay, the wreck is slightly off-centre to the left, a few yards out from the shore and just to the left of the exit of a stream which runs down to the cove under the tiny wooden bridge which you cross to continue on to Bolt Head. That dark shape underwater is not rocks, but all that is left of that once tall ship, the *Herzogin Cecilie*.

Dependent, of course, on weather conditions, you will often see a diving boat anchored over her, for there is enough wreckage left to interest divers amid the growths and weed which festoon her.

It is interesting to note that while the name for the bay is now Starehole, it was originally called Stair Hole, probably because of the steepness of the track up which seaweed for manuring was carried from the shore to East Soar Farm further inland.

The coastal path continues on right to Bolt Tail and passes the Hamstone off Soar Mill Cove, which the ship struck first of all. Be warned, however, the going is hard with steep descents both into and out of Soar Mill Cove, not to mention the climb up to Bolt Head itself which is now just ahead of you. From Bolt Head to Bolt Tail there are five miles of wonderful cliff scenery, all National Trust property, but it is not for anyone unused to walking long distances.

CHAPTER SEVEN

Ramillies

The date: February 15th, 1760.
The weather: appalling.

The greatest disaster ever recorded in the annals of the Royal Navy was about to occur. Out of 734 men on board the 90-gun warship *Ramillies*, only 26 were to survive her wrecking at the foot of the 300-foot high granite cliffs of Bolt Tail, South Devon.

The hurricane that was the cause of it all struck Southern England on February 14th. Trees were torn up, houses lost their roofs, haystacks disappeared and even whole cottages were blown down. In London, a complete stack of chimneys came down in Newcastle Court, near Grosvenor Square. The lead was ripped off the house of Earl Cowper in Great George Street. The whole gable end of a house in Hanover Street crashed to the ground. A pinnacle of a building adjoining the House of Commons crashed through the roof of Parliament just over the Speaker's chair. More than 27 feet of lead on the Admiralty's roof was rolled up like a scroll.

The Mall was blocked by branches ripped from trees. Great thunder claps, lightning flashes, hail, rain and sleet added to the damage as the storm roared on. In every harbour in Southern England, ships were smashed and sailors drowned. At sea, conditions were so appalling that ships either ran before the wind with bare poles, or struggled desperately to find any sort of shelter from the stormy blasts.

7   The grave of *Ramillies*

Ramillies was out there and in desperate trouble in mid-Channel somewhere off the Brittany peninsula. We don't know exactly where she was when the first of the storms hit her but she must have been well out towards the Atlantic. She had sailed from Plymouth on February 6th with the rest of the Channel Squadron, under the command of Admiral Edward Boscawen. His orders were to join the rest of the Fleet in Quiberon Bay, and Boscawen was impatient to get there. His two previous attempts had failed due to bad weather and strong westerly winds, and despite winds that were still unfavourable he set sail once again.

The Admiral was in his flag-ship, the *Royal William*. In addition to *Ramillies*, his squadron consisted of the *Sandwich*, *St. George*, *Princess Amelia*, a frigate, the *Venus*, and a cutter called *Hawke*. Together they fought their way down the Channel. By the 12th they were facing a freshening south-westerly. Squalls of rain and sleet made the continuous altering of sails a misery for all aboard. Then in came the fore-runners of the hurricane. Gales tore at them and swung from south-west to north-west and back again. The gales were "so violent" wrote Boscawen later, "that I could seldom carry a topsail" and on the night of the 13th February, they were obliged to lie-to with bare masts. On the 14th the wind increased from the south-west, so much so that the *Royal William* had all her sails split, was repeatedly pooped by huge seas and suffered severe damage to parts of her decking.

It says a great deal for the seamanship of *Ramillies'* captain, who bore the strange name of Wittewronge Taylor, that up until that point *Ramillies* had stayed with the flagship. *Ramillies* was long past her prime and was leaking badly.

Launched at Portsmouth in 1749, she had been Admiral Byng's flagship in the engagement off Minorca as a result of which he was shot for cowardice on the quarterdeck. She took part in many of the naval actions of the Seven Years' War, but missed the great triumph of the campaign, the Battle of Quiberon Bay, because she was even then leaking so much that Admiral Sir Edward Hawke had to move his flag from her only a few days before the action. Captain Wittewronge Taylor, Hawke's flag captain, stayed with *Ramillies* and was her captain to her end and his. Those leaks were meant to have been repaired during her stay in Plymouth, but out in those huge seas sweeping in from the Atlantic she was leaking again. And not a little either.

All hands were at the pumps and teams of men with buckets were baling too. One of her timbers seemed to have given and she was making water so fast that Captain Taylor ordered the shot taken out of some of the guns and lights made ready so that they could fire the guns and hoist the lights to signal their distress. It was now the evening of February 14th, 1760.

The reason those distress signals were not given tells us a great deal about the discipline of the Navy of that time. There seems to have been some sort of consultation on board *Ramillies* between the captain, the senior officers and the sailing master. Their conclusion: it would be better to bear away without making the signal of distress "as some other of the squadron might take it to be the Admiral". And that would never do!

So *Ramillies*, despite the water slopping about in her holds and the desperate pumping and baling going on, hoisted a foresail and drew away from the flagship into the darkness. All that night she ran up Channel with a south-westerly hurricane behind her. When the dawn came her crew could see little more than in the night. Spray, squalls of rain which stung exposed skin like wasps, and seas so big that a whole ship could have been hidden from view in any of the troughs between them made any sight of land impossible.

By ten in the morning of the 15th, none aboard *Ramillies* had the slightest idea where they were. They seemed to be in a giant white mist of water from out of which massive waves reared up astern of them, hung threateningly above their poop before the 90 mile per hour winds tore the tops off them, and then with a sickening lurch the ship wallowed back into the trough left by the walls of water passing under them. It was clear, as *Ramillies* took longer and longer to rise out of these troughs, that the pumps were no longer keeping pace with the water coming in. Unless she found shelter soon, she was likely to founder.

For one moment there came a lull in the wind and as the spray dropped away one of the midshipmen shouted "Land-ho!", but by the time all eyes on deck had followed his pointing finger the gap was gone and only one or two other officers were agreed that there had been something that looked like land on their port bow. Anything it seems was better than nothing and so the sailing master had the mainsail set and headed the ship to the north-east.

He had not seen the land himself and was not convinced that anyone else had, but unless the compass was useless and the wind had swung during the night, he knew that such a course must in the end bring them a landfall. He held the course for over half-an-hour and was beginning to wonder if they were in the Channel at all, when suddenly he too had a glimpse of what was unmistakeably the shape of an island off the main shore. Before the visibility clamped down again, the master had identified it as Looe Island. He was much relieved by this as it meant he was still to the westward of Plymouth and the shelter of the Sound was not too far away.

Unfortunately the sailing master of the *Ramillies* was totally and utterly wrong. He had got the wrong island. What he had seen was Burgh Island at the entrance to the Avon at Bantham. He was 26 miles further to the east than he thought. Worse, he was well within the great sweep at Bigbury Bay and was caught on a lee shore with a giant south-westerly blowing him to disaster!

From the moment of that decision the end of *Ramillies* was almost inevitable. Almost, but not quite. The one chance of saving the ship would have been to have stayed in Bigbury Bay, perhaps by anchoring, until the wind had blown itself out.

But the sailing master did no such thing. In fact he made another decision which further sealed the *Ramillies'* fate. He decided to try and round what he thought was Rame Head and get into the shelter of Plymouth Sound. But it wasn't the Rame Head. It was the great towering cliffs of the Bolt, cliffs which run for five miles in massive majesty to Bolt Head and the entrance to Salcombe Harbour and he could never have got the *Ramillies* across the Bar and into shelter there.

It is important here to know that the sailing master in those days was in command of the actual sailing of the ship, under direction of the captain, and many decisions were taken by him on his own authority. This decision to round what he thought was Rame Head was, it seems, left to him, though there is evidence that the Captain and some other officers disagreed with him. But not apparently strongly enough.

By now the ship had been seen from the land. Looking down on her from the heights of Bolt Tail the crowd that gathered there could see her struggling in great seas, at one moment lifted high on a crest then disappearing in a cloud of spray in the trough.

It is likely that most of the able-bodied population of nearby Hope would have struggled up the cliffs despite the howling winds. So valuable to the ordinary people was a wreck that as many as ten thousand people would gather on the Devon coast when a ship was trapped in a bay in such bad weather. As the ship moved back and forth attempting to claw her way out to the open sea, so the crowds would move along with her.

Those who watched *Ramillies* would have been disappointed that she was a warship. Navy ships provided poor pickings when compared with a merchantman driven on shore. But Navy ship or not, so poor was the average person that any wreck was better than none. At worst she could provide wood for burning or, better still, building.

Those crowds who watched from Bolt Tail and any neighbouring high ground such as Bigbury itself, were, even if they thought of a wreck as fair game, surprised to see *Ramillies* set all sails, even including her topsails, and attempt to run to eastward. They could see that the great swells hitting the base of the cliffs and showering them with spray would, without doubt, push and suck the ship into her grave.

The sailing master realised his mistake too late. Too late, he changed his mind and attempted to stay the ship, but the wind carried her on. So strong was it that it was using her masts and flapping sails as leverage and pushing her into those savage rocks.

Now Captain Wittewronge Taylor seems to have snatched back command of his ship from the sailing master. "Let go the main-sheet", he shouted and two sailors, William Wise and Robuck, did as they were ordered. But it was too late again. Whether the main-mast was cut away to reduce windage or snapped, we don't know, but we do know that within minutes it was gone and so was the mizzenmast. Now the people on the cliffs were looking right down on *Ramillies*, only 400 yards from Bolt Tail. Some idea of the conditions for those on board is given by the statement from one of the survivors that at this moment "the weather was so thick that as yet they did not know the land". Perhaps he meant that they did not know what part of the coast they were approaching, as no one could have missed those cliffs towering over them.

At this moment William Wise heard the sailing master give the command "Let go the anchor and clew up forward". This was done, but for some reason the anchor stuck and hurriedly the smaller bow anchor was cut loose and both anchors fell together. Both cables raced out, but crossed one another. Even so the anchors brought the ship bow to wind and to a halt. Any hope of sailing the *Ramillies* out of her fix was abandoned and the foremast was cut down. As it went it carried away the bowsprit with it. By now it was 2 o'clock in the afternoon. For a while it looked as though *Ramillies* would be held in her position.

But the wind increased by the minute. "I think from the hour of two in the afternoon, it blew stronger than I ever felt it in my life," wrote Admiral Boscawen later.

That wind blew *St. George* and the *Venus* all the way back to Spithead! The *Hawke* simply disappeared forever with all hands.

Ramillies held to her anchors until just before dusk when the two anchor cables, sawing violently across each other at each jerk of a wave, finally parted. Nothing could stop her now, she swung round broadside with the next great swell. Down went the sheet anchor, but they couldn't let out enough cable before her starboard side struck the rocks. Her bow ground round and she was in the crushing machine between the waves and the cliffs.

Walls of water swept over her. The Captain of Marines went off his head and marched up and down the poop singing and declaiming. The boatswain had brought his young son to sea with him and now tried to save the child's life by flinging him on to the rocks, only to see the child's brains dashed out. Seconds later the boatswain's lifeless body joined that of his son in the surf.

Men struggled screaming to jump off the ship on to the rocks. Most were flung to their deaths like straws as the waves smashed them high up the sheer cliff-face.

Only 26 men managed to get some sort of grip and drag themselves into crevices and cracks in the rock in which the waves could not reach them.

William Wise was the last man to get away. He let down the starboard stern ladder, scrambled down the ropes and threw himself on to the rocks. A wave lifted the ship and smashed part of it down on his right leg, turning most of it into bloody pulp. Despite this he got up and hopped and dragged himself up a small gully away from the sea. When he looked back, the ship was gone. It had completely disappeared, all that was left were pieces like firewood floating about in the froth. And everywhere were the bloody mangled bodies of his shipmates and each wave flung more of them at the cliffs. William Wise turned away and started to drag himself tuft by tuft of vegetation up the gully which he hoped would lead him away from the sea and up to safety. He hadn't got very far before it became completely dark ...

How to get there

To reach the spot from which you can look down on the grave of *Ramillies* you should drive along the A381 from Kingsbridge, a good if narrow undulating road, for about two-and-a-half miles. Clearly signposted "Hope Cove" on your right is an even narrower lane which leads down to both Inner and Outer Hope. In the summer holiday season, this road carries a good deal of traffic, but there are many passing places and most drivers are courteous. (Ordnance Survey Sheet 202.)

Parking at Inner Hope from which we start our walk up the cliffs is very restricted and you will find it best to use the main car park at Outer Hope. Inner Hope is only a few moments walk from there towards Bolt Tail, which you can't miss towering over the village. Don't be confused by those names. Inner Hope is not as it sounds at the back of Outer Hope. Inner Hope really gets its name from the fact that it is closer in to the headland of Bolt Tail.

Continue round the little bay of Hope Cove itself until you come to a small slipway right under the cliffs. Just beside the slipway a gate leads the way on to National Trust property. You can't miss it – it is the obvious way to start walking up to Bolt Tail, and once again it is clearly signposted as a Public Footpath. (Ordnance Survey Sheet SX 63 NE, six inches to the mile will be useful now, but your motoring map Sheet 202 will also help to appreciate the great sweep of coastline you are going to see).

Though our walk is going to take us up some 300 feet, it is not a violent climb and is easily managed. At first the path takes you through some low woodland and when you emerge from the overhanging bushes, you will see you have a choice of paths up to the crest of Bolt Tail. You can take either. The one to your right takes you around the curve of Bolt Tail. The path directly ahead is a steeper climb, but leads more directly to the top.

The best for our purpose is to take the right-hand path. As you approach the westward tip of Bolt Tail, look back and if the sun is shining you will have a marvellous view of Hope and some of the most beautiful coastal scenery in the whole of Britain. Close in are the white cottages and houses of Hope contrasting with the pale blue, almost transparent, sea. Those black rocks jutting out from Hope are of particular interest. The big long one with grass on top is the Shippen Rock, the site of an Armada wreck and one that is the subject of the next chapter.

Look further to the west and you can see the natural arch of Thurlestone Rock and beyond that the modern houses on the Mead which are from this viewpoint in front of the beautiful thatched cottages of the village of Thurlestone. Further still is the mouth of the Avon at Bantham and Burgh Island, which *Ramillies* mistook for Looe Island which is 26 miles further to the west near Plymouth. The entrance to Plymouth Sound is among those very distant headlands.

Burgh Island is easly spotted if the tide is low by its distinctive causeway of yellow sand sweeping out to it. At low tide you can walk out to the island and its excellent pub.

That great sweep of water to the westward of you is Bigbury Bay, which, though it doesn't look a great deal like an enclosed bay, has in fact been the scene of countless wrecks of sailing ships trapped by south-westerly gales on a lee shore.

Now to find *Ramillies*. Some indication of the extent of the disaster and the shock it gave the nation – reports appeared in

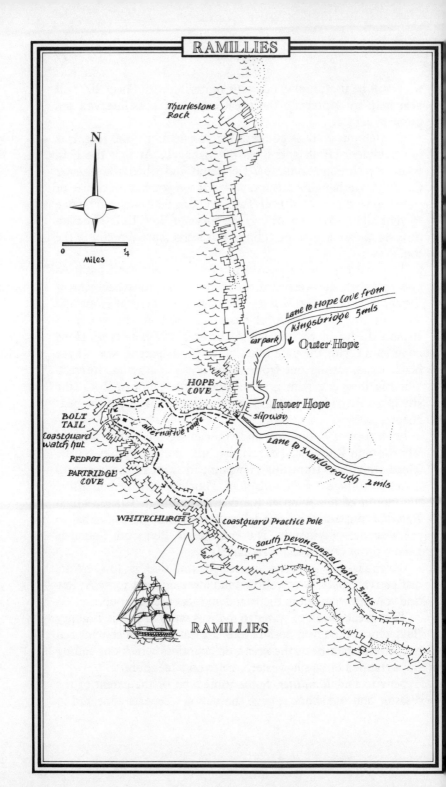

RAMILLIES

Thurlestone Rock

N

0 ¼
Miles

Lane to Hope Cove from
Kingsbridge 5 mls

car park

Outer Hope

HOPE
COVE

Inner Hope

slipway

BOLT
TAIL

alternative route

Coastguard
watch hut

Lane to Marlborough 2 mls

REDROT COVE

PARTRIDGE
COVE

WHITECHURCH

coastguard Practice Pole

south Devon Coastal Path 5mls

RAMILLIES

all the publications of the time – is the fact that you will find
Ramillies Cove even on today's Ordnance survey maps. It has
been called that ever since the wreck. Which is strange because
whoever marked it got the wrong place! I know because I have
dived among her cannon, and she is definitely not at the spot
marked "Ramillies" on today's maps. True she is only two
coves away to the east, but here we will get it right.

Follow the lower path leading to the east just under the crest
of the cliffs. A broader path goes along the top and that might
be a quicker way – and safer on a really windy day. Put your
dog on a lead and do not leave the path or go down the grassy
slopes for a better view – you may not be able to stop when you
want to!

The lower path leads beneath the Coastguard Lookout on
the tip of Bolt Tail and is narrow.

After the deep red rocks of Redtrot Cove and the deep
chasm of Partridge Cove, soon the path will lead you round the
identation called Whitechurch and climbs up to a small peak.
From this spot the path goes down and across a grass and
bracken area, which seems to swoop down towards the sea.
Sticking out of the right centre of this grassy area and slightly
below your position on the path is a grey rocky outcrop. It is
small but the only one in the area so you can't miss it. Some 50
yards on from this outcrop and you are standing right over the
grave of *Ramillies*. You may well look down and see a diving
boat anchored below you for this is a popular site for Britain's
skin-divers.

You are now standing over the very spot and in the same
place from which all those people from the village looked
down on the wreck in 1760. You are also standing on the very
spot from which Admiral Boscawen's special envoy, Benjamin
Hall, one of the Master Attendants of Plymouth Dockyard,
tried desperately to see what could be saved from the wreck.
He had also been sent by the Admiral to see that any survivors
did not escape from the Navy's grasp!

For some reason he stayed the night at Thurlestone, not
Hope, and sent this letter to the Admiral in Plymouth:

Thurlestone,
Feb. 17-1760

Honourable Sir,

At one this afternoon I got to the place where the ship was lost which is a litel to the Eastward of the Bolt Tail in the dismal spot that fate designed her – She is entireley under water and what comes from her no boat can ventur to save yet as the sea is very high but as the wind is at N.W. hope tomorrow at low water to take up all the Ironwork and gather things that comes on shore and give it to the care of the officers of the Customs. I cant see aney part of her, mast sails or yards soe I think the sea has split and torn them to pieces without they lay in coves that I cant see without a boat – this evening I went to the village where some of the seamen was that was saved and told them the Admirals orders they that are able gave me there word of coming to Dartm. tomorrow and those that are lame ask me how there landlords is to be paid to that I can give no answer – Sir I hope what I shale doe tomorrow will meet with your aprobation to sound in her as the guns is faling in her hole and the Fishermen told me at low water its three fathom I shale take wot step I can to preserve all the stores I can and wait your Honble Command.

I am Sir your most obedient Humble servant to command.

BENJ. HALL

Together with that letter from Benjamin Hall there is another one carefully preserved in the Public Record Office at Kew. This one is from two men who also stood where you are standing now – Frank Shepherd and Thomas Barriball, Customs men who were stationed at Hope. They had been on watch on the cliff-top until the wreck occurred and were still on watch as they wrote: "in order to prevent the Country People plundering his Majesty's stores. This day in conjunction with Mr. Hall we have agreed to hire eight men to bring the iron worke and what else may be found up the steep cliff,

being in our opinion the only expedient that is practicable
… we shall do every thing in our power that may be conducive
to his Majesty's service …"

From your position on the path you can understand
Benjamin Hall's difficulty and how it was that he could not see
right down to the sea. Do not be tempted to work your way
down from the path. The cliff falls away suddenly even if the
first part looks a gentle slope. You could not in fact get any
closer to the bow of *Ramillies* than you are now for as Hall
later reported to Boscawen – "The stem is drove into a cave to
the eastward …" And I can tell you, from diving on her, that
underwater right inside the red-roofed cave is the best
preserved of the only three cannon known to remain on the
seabed. Cannonballs lie in encrusted groups and under some
rocks is a big piece of spongy wood.

It seems that most of the cannon were salvaged at the time
and it must have been a mammoth task to haul those heavy
guns up the cliff. One doubts if the eight hired men could do it,
but no doubt most of the men in the village were used as
muscle power from time to time.

Are you sure you are in the right place? Well, you can check
that very simply. If you continue along the path to the east it
will take you up to join the main path which has been
travelling parallel with the lower one along the crest of the
cliffs. It is here as the two come together that the area opens
out into some tufty grass, well scored with rabbit diggings and
droppings. A short distance further on you will see a white
mast with footholds like steps up to its sliced off top. This is
exactly what it is meant to look like – a mast. It was used by
the Coastguards for rocket apparatus practice. The lines were
fired by rocket at the mast and then, by means of the steps,
secured to the top as though by a wrecked crew. It is *not* a
navigational mark. It is, however, a good mark for the
Ramillies. If you reach it you've gone too far.

However, before we finally leave the scene of the wreck,
look around at the depressions or pits in the surface at the very
top of the cliffs. One of these was known for years as William
Wise's Pit. Remember that we had left that seaman with a

shattered leg dragging himself up the cliff. Well, William Wise survived. He was found in one of those pits the next morning and carried down to Hope. Perhaps he was one of those in Benjamin Hall's letter who was asking how his landlord was going to be paid. Which pit is the actual one? Unfortunately everyone locally gives you a different answer. Take your pick of the pits!

You now have a choice. If you intend to walk on by the coastal path around one of the most magnificent stretches of scenery in Devon, be warned. It is five miles and can be very tiring.

On the other hand I cannot show you one of the cannon salvaged from the *Ramillies* even if you return to Hope. It lies at the top of the Shippen Rock in Outer Hope, rusting amid the grass, after being salvaged in 1906. Sadly you cannot walk up to see it because private land now bars the way. But do not grieve - when you are looking at the Shippen you are looking at the only known Armada wreck site on the English mainland. But that's for the next chapter.

CHAPTER EIGHT

San Pedro

The date: October 28th, 1588.
The weather: south-westerly gales and then more gales.

A Spanish Armada ship, the *San Pedro el Mayor*, is out of control as the men aboard have not enough strength left to handle the sails, and strikes the Shippen Rocks in Hope Cove, South Devon. She is the only Armada ship known to have been wrecked in England.

Despite the fact that she carried 30 cannon, the *San Pedro el Mayor*, or St. Peter the Great, was no fighting ship. She was one of the Squadron of Urcas, which were the transports and supply ships of the Armada.

The *San Pedro* was fitted out as a hospital ship, one of 23 transports listed in the Armada inventory made at Lisbon on May 20th, 1588. Her cannon were for defence, not offence, and so she left Spain with 30 sailors and 100 soldiers aboard. Fifty more men were aboard to organise the hospital and tend the sick and wounded in it.

The Squadron of Urcas was commanded by Juan Gomez de Medina and he led this cumbersome collection of ships from his flagship, the *Gran Grifon*.

The *San Pedro* was a smaller ship than the *Gran Grifon* and was about 580 tons by today's standards of ship measurement.

We know quite a lot about the early part of the *San Pedro's* voyage. She is reported as being there, off Plymouth, inside the safety of the Armada's great crescent-shaped battle formation, when the first skirmishes with the English took place on July 21st, 1588. Skirmishes is perhaps the wrong word for the early naval battles as by Wednesday, August 3rd, the Armada was taking a terrible pounding from English cannon. One Spanish ship, for example, was seen to have blood running out of the scupper pipes into the sea. And the commander of *San Pedro's* squadron, Juan Gomez de Medina didn't escape unscathed either. He received the personal attention of Francis Drake, when he was unwise enough to let his flagship, *Gran Grifon*, get a little behind one of the tips of the Spanish formation.

Drake swooped with all sails bent to take advantage of the light wind near Portland Bill. The *Gran Grifon* saw the danger and struggled to rejoin the Spanish line. She was too late. Drake put *Revenge* on broadside course, gave her every gun, came about and gave her the other broadside. Then raked her again as he ran at "half musket shot" distance from her stern.

Seventy men on *Gran Grifon* were either killed or wounded and her decks were slippery with blood. A contemporary report says that she took 70 cannonballs in her hull, but was finally able to rejoin the main Spanish force. Of those wounded men, some were certainly transferred to the *San Pedro* and the *Gran Grifon* was repaired at Gravelines. Then the Armada sailed on into more battles until finally they were forced to flee through the North Sea and up to the very tip of Scotland.

Now the only way home was to go round Scotland and down the west coast of Ireland. The *San Pedro* lurched on after her commander in the *Gran Grifon* as the Armada steered westward between the Orkneys and the Shetlands.

On the night of August 20th, the Armada passed between Ronaldsay and Fair Isle, but neither the *San Pedro* or the *Gran Grifon* was with them. Fierce squalls had ripped at the lumbering transports and split them from the main force. Now the *Gran Grifon* found herself with five ships, but the *San Pedro* was not one of them. She was somewhere out there alone in huge seas, fighting headwinds that pushed her hither and thither despite the efforts of the crew. Juan Gomez de Medina in *Gran Grifon* was wrecked on Fair Isle and survived. The

8   Shippen Rocks, showing where the *San Pedro* was wrecked

San Pedro was not so lucky; her struggle against the sea had only just begun.

The Duke of Medina Sidonia, commanding the Armada from his flagship, the *San Martin de Portugal*, had, when he had been in touch with his ships, ordered his captains not to seek shelter in Irish ports for he feared that any who did would meet with no quarter. Some, we know from other wrecks, defied his orders – some as their last chance, others because they could not help themselves.

The *San Pedro* was in as bad a way as any of the other ships and there is some evidence that she, too, defied her orders and ventured into the port of Vicey, County Kerry, to try and pick up fresh water and shelter from the endless westerly gales. Her water barrels were foul. One report said that the water was so stinking and full of growths that they had to strain it through their teeth to get any liquid at all!

However, supplies or not, the *San Pedro* had to sail again. She did – into more gales. The continual battle with the sea took its toll of crew and soldiers alike and fewer and fewer of the men had the strength to handle the ship. Some idea of the effect of these conditions on the sick and wounded below decks is a report that some of the more seriously wounded drowned in the water which swilled back and forth below decks.

Finally, the *San Pedro* was out of control. The winds blew her whichever way they chose and after a three-month voyage, during which she had circumnavigated the British Isles, she was back where her troubles had started – off Plymouth!

With not enough men left on their feet to set sail or haul down, a south-westerly gale picked her up and blew her straight towards the very heart of her enemies, Plymouth Sound. Then the wind shifted slightly and she came into Bigbury Bay. On and on, and then, as though committing suicide, straight into Hope Cove. And there on October 28th, 1588, her misery ended. Soon she was a complete wreck on the Shippen Rocks and the looting and pillaging was about to begin.

I say about to begin, because if you look at the Shippen today you will see that determined men could clamber over its grassy back and down almost to the rocky tip. But on that wild day in October they couldn't do that. Huge seas were breaking right over the Shippen and the wreck, driven on by that monstrous south-westerly gale.

And if the Spaniards on board the *San Pedro* were too weak to handle the ship, this does not mean that they were too weak to set about saving themselves and, in some cases, their belongings. We know that some managed to get ashore despite the storm.

We know this because of a letter in the Public Record Office in the Calendar of State Papers (Domestic) for 1588 from a man who was actually on the scene soon after the wreck. He wrote a report to the Privy Council, dating it November 5th, 1588, from his home at Cockington, near Torquay. His name was George Cary, he was a Deputy-Lieutenant of Devon, and he had been staying at Plymouth when the news of the wreck reached him ...

"... And during my abode there, having understanding that one of the Spanish fleet was cast on shore at a place called Hope and the great pilfering and spoils that the country people made, I rode thither and took order for the restoring and rehaving again of all such things as either by search or inquiry I could find out and have put the same in inventory. And took order, for the orderly saving of the rest, as weather would give leave, to have the same on land, appointing two head constables to attend that service, and they and others to keep several inventories.

"The ship is a hulk, and called *St. Peter the Great*, one of those two ships appointed for the hospital of the whole Navy. She is in burden, as they say, 550 tons, but I think not so much.

"The ship is not to be recovered; she lieth on a rock, and full of water to her upper decks. They confess that there were put into her, at her coming out of Spain, thirty mariners, one hundred soldiers, fifty appertaining to the hospital. There are now remaining about 140, or thereabouts".

A staggering statement and one that tells us more about the *San Pedro's* ghastly last voyage than anything else. Forty of her crew had gone and it sounds as though none of the sick and wounded put into her could have survived.

But Cary had not finished: "There was put into her as much

drugs and pothecary stuff as came to 6,000 ducats, of which I think there will come little good of the same, the weather such as none could get aboard. There has been some plate and certain ducats rifled and spoiled at their first landing, both from their persons and out of their chests".

So some did get ashore and if they had their chests with them, they must have come ashore by boat or raft. Certainly you will see how important this detail is when we come to walk the ground and I tell you where coins are still to be found!

Cary seemed upset at this plundering of the survivors and seems to pooh-pooh the idea that there is much else to be gained from the wreck: "The ship, I think, will prove of no great value; the ordnance is all iron, and no brass; their ground tackle all spent, save only one new cable. There are no men of account in the ship, soldiers and such as have risen by service, and bestowed all their wealth in this action".

No men of account means that there was no one survivor who would be worth ransom money and the fact that all "their ground tackle" was gone means that at least the *San Pedro* had tried anchoring somewhere to save herself. Perhaps it was on the Book Rocks off Thurlestone Sands because divers have seen great anchors there.

You will note also that Cary does not specify which rock the *San Pedro* struck. It is, however, significant that the Shippen Rock's name can only have come from "ship in" or "ship on" and I can trace no record of any earlier reference to this name before the wreck of the *San Pedro*.

It may be that from reading Cary's letter you will think him a mean man, concerned only with the value of the wreck. In that case you should know that while 120 of the survivors were crammed into one building in the locality (where exactly we do not know) and were given some food, twenty of the officers were kept apart. Ten of these were sent into Kingsbridge. Cary himself took the apothecary and the surgeon into his own home at Cockington. The remaining eight officers were taken to Ilton Castle, the residence of Sir William Courtenay, the third Earl of Devon and High Sheriff of Devonshire, who was later to marry Sir Francis Drake's widow.

And Cary, for all his cares about money, assigned to each prisoner one penny per day out of his private means until "the pleasure of Her Majesty's Privy Council be made known".

That pleasure was not long in coming. All the prisoners were to be executed! Fortunately for the Spaniards this order was quickly countermanded and the prisoners were put in charge of Anthony Ashley, who was clerk to the Privy Council. He took up residence with Sir William Courtenay at Ilton Castle as soon as he could. He moved swiftly because his letter to the Privy Council is dated November 12th, 1588. It was written at Ilton and begins: "May it please Your Lordships", and then goes on to say that he has made an inventory of the goods saved from the vessel, and continues:

"The ship being run upon rocks by the Spaniards, is now through the tempestuous weather broken in pieces and scattered on the seashore, and order is taken for the saving of such things as are anything worth".

What finally happened to all the prisoners we don't know, but the wreck site can be clearly seen today.

How to get there

The Shippen Rock divides Outer Hope from Inner Hope. Grass grows right up to the top, but access today to the crest is barred by a line of houses across the foot. The Shippen, too, separates the two beaches of Hope. Outer Hope beach is known as Mouthwell and Inner Hope beach is described as Hope Cove and is inside the breakwater which protects the harbour.

The best view of the Shippen is obtained from the cliff path which leads up to the National Trust property of Bolt Tail (see previous chapter about the *Ramillies* wreck). Looking down from here you can see clearly how the wind would have driven

the *San Pedro* to her doom on the Shippen, but you need to see
the same place in a storm and south-westerly gale to realise
how violent the seas can be on that tongue of rock.

In such a wind any boats or rafts getting away from the
wreck would also have been driven across the little bay of
Inner Hope until they reached the shore right under the
towering cliffs of Bolt Tail.

In fact we know that is what happened to the Spanish
survivors and for the reason that we know it we must go back
to Cary's letter – "There has been some plate and certain
ducats rifled and spoiled at their first landing, both from their
persons and out of their chests".

Imagine the scene. The Spaniards stagger ashore, stumbling
through the surf, to be met not by helping hands, but by a
rapacious mob of people from roundabouts, to whom such a
wreck was a wonderful gift of God. Such a wreck could
provide enough goods and loot to keep them in plenty for at
least a year. To understand this you must realise the penury in
which most people lived in those days. Even a piece of timber
was worth a great deal. A gold or silver coin was riches beyond
belief. So when the Spaniards came ashore, Cary's description
of "certain ducats rifled and spoiled" is the understatement of
all time. What clothes they had were torn off them and
probably torn apart as the mob fought each other for posses-
sion.

Come now down to the start of that cliff path. The old
building just where the path starts is the former lifeboat
station. Just in front of it is the old lifeboat slipway. Here it is
that the Spaniards came ashore. We know that because from
time to time ancient Spanish coins are found on the beach just
by the end of the slipway. They are extremely unlikely to have
been washed right over from the Shippen and the wreck. No,
these coins were undoubtedly dropped and trodden into the
beach during the looting described by Cary, or maybe fell from
the Spaniards' clothing as they fought their way through the
surf to safety.

Several have been found over the years and bear on one side
the Maltese cross and on the other Philip of Spain's coat of

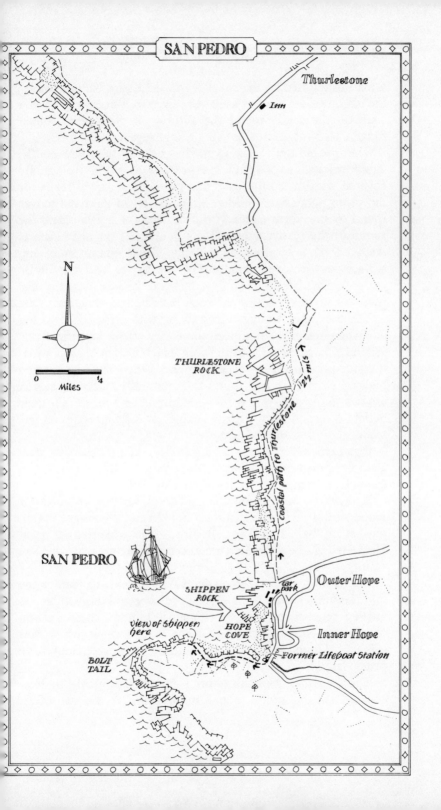

arms surmounted by the royal crown. Most are badly worn by the action of the sea. So keep your eyes well peeled when you walk on the sand around the slipway. A Salcombe woman found two coins on such a walk. What happened was this:

The prevailing winds over the British Isles are south-westerlies and as a result the beaches at Hope are usually covered with the sort of sand that provides plenty of scope for the young sandcastle-builder. However, when the wind moves round to the north-east and blows hard for a few tides, the action of the sea changes and the fine sand from the beach is removed by a scouring movement. Great quantities of top surface are removed temporarily out to sea and the under surface of the beach is exposed. Beneath the sand is a stiff clay base. It is in this clay that the coins have been discovered.

The Salcombe woman was walking with a friend on such a day when one of them noticed something sticking up out of the ground. It was the edge of the coin which caught her eye when the sun glinted on it for a moment. When the two women realised what they had found they naturally began to search around the spot to see if they could find any more. To their delight a second coin, slightly smaller, was found within a few feet of their first silver discovery.

Other coins have been found from time to time, usually after a similar north-easterly blow. But if you don't find a coin, you can still see some other relics of the shipwreck.

A pleasant walk along the cliff path starting from Outer Hope will bring you to Thurlestone. Here in the village inn, in the saloon bar, a notice will direct your attention to great blackened old beams which are said to have come from the *San Pedro*.

And a short drive away in the Cookworthy Museum in the Old Grammar School at 108 Fore Street, Kingsbridge, is another relic of the wreck – a Spanish helmet. There too you can see an old photograph of some body armour which was originally found with the helmet, but that seems to have disappeared.

There is little doubt that this 16th century Spanish helmet comes from the wreck, though it was found in the wall of St.

Andrew's Church in the nearby village of Aveton Gifford during repairs in 1800.

A strange place for it to be found? Not really. Remember Cary's letter ... "I rode thither and took order for the restoring and rehaving again of all such things ... appointing two head constables to attend that service ..."

What a panic to get rid of any loot there must have been when Cary and his two constables got to work. The wreck belonged to the Crown and anyone caught with Crown property, stolen Crown property at that, would have been hung without doubt. A hole in a church wall would have been as good a dumping place as any, probably better, as Cary and his constables were hardly likely to go so far as to search churches!

CHAPTER NINE

Coronation

The date: September 3rd, 1691.
The weather: "Verry Squally Stormy" noted the log-keeper of the *Royal Oak*, but in fact there was a violent gale blowing from the south-south-east.

The *Royal Oak* survived, but some 600 men of the Royal Navy were about to die within sight of Plymouth Sound and safety when their Majesties' ship *Coronation* capsized. Only 22 men were saved, washed ashore clinging to wreckage.

During the spring and summer of 1691, the combined English and Dutch fleets did their damnedest to lure the French out of the Channel ports into a stand-up battle, but the "Frenchies" were not to be drawn. The English fleet drew up plans to go in after them, but thought better of it and patrolled endlessly up and down the Channel hoping against hope that some French admiral would have a rush of blood to the head and chase out after them.

Wisely, in view of the weather – a bad spring was followed by a worse summer – the French stayed put. The English fleet sheltered in Torbay on August 23rd and Captain Charles Skelton commanding *Coronation* was probably glad of the rest for both himself and his ship.

It is the *Royal Oak's* log and that of other ships in the Fleet, now safely preserved in the Public Record Office, which tell us that there was now a change in the weather. The English sailed out again to resume patrolling in what the log-keeper of the

9   Lady Cove, Penlee Point

10   The Grotto at Penlee Point

Royal Oak called "All Continuing faire and Pleasant Weather. At 8 of ye Clock this morning the West End of ye Lizard Bore NWBW 6 Leagues".

But before the *Coronation* reached the Lizard a strange incident took place. She must have entered Falmouth Bay, hove-to, and launched one of her longboats. Sitting in the stern seats as the men bent to their oars or as the little sail was hoisted was Mr. William Passinger, First Lieutenant of *Coronation*. His orders were to collect fresh water and provisions from Falmouth.

Why *Coronation* needed fresh water and provisions within a week of sailing from Torbay anchorage we shall never know. The fact that only one longboat was sent suggests that they were special requirements for the Captain's table. But it seems distinctly odd to send such an important fellow as the First Lieutenant on such a mission.

It seems even odder when you know that Lieutenant Passinger never completed his mission. Before he could get back, *Coronation* sailed without him.

Captain Skelton was an experienced man who would not have failed to provision his ship in Torbay and one longboat would never have coped with the demands of the whole ship. Perhaps the water-butts were foul and the Captain wanted fresh sweet water for himself and not his crew. It seems unlikely for Captain Charles Skelton, from his record, was not that kind of man. His conduct at the attack on the Dutch Smyrna Fleet in March 1672 when he was second lieutenant on board the *Gloucester* had been noted as "highly approved". He fought bravely at the Battle of Sole Bay the same year and was given his first command, the *Speedwell*, on February 5th, 1673. From then on the only way his career had gone was up. Command followed command until in 1690 he was made captain of *Coronation*. This promotion seems to have met with approval all round, even by the ordinary seamen in her, for he was not known as a man who kept discipline by flogging his orders home.

Coronation was a fine ship and indeed was the flagship of Sir Ralph Delavall, Vice Admiral of the Blue (the rear squadron) at the Battle of Beachy Head on June 30th, 1690. For five hours *Coronation*, under Skelton's command, and with Sir Ralph aboard, fought a much larger force of the French fleet. Once again Skelton's captaincy was without reproach.

Coronation had been launched in 1685. She was listed as a second-rate man o'war of 1366 tons with provision for a crew of 660 men. One hundred and forty feet long and with a beam of 44 feet 9 inches, she carried 90 guns, ranging from 6-pounders up to massive 32-pounders. Fully laden she drew some 18 feet of water.

Whether Lieutenant Passinger looked out of Falmouth and saw her sail away or whether he rowed out to find her gone we do not know, but gone she certainly was. That August was a wicked month and, though on Monday, August 31st, *Coronation* was off Ushant in "continuing faire weather and easy Gailes", during the night of that last day of the month the weather changed dramatically. The first of September was "squally, blowing very fresh" and the next day it was worse – "squally freshening weather".

In the early hours of the morning the Fleet turned back for the shelter of Plymouth. Pushed by the winds which were at gale force and coming directly from the south, the great ships of the Channel Fleet raced for Plymouth. Now the wind swung to south-west and strengthened even more, forcing all the ships to take in canvas. Finally the wind made up its mind, settled in the south-south-west and blew at close to hurricane strength.

The trap was set. The captains had to make up their minds. Ahead lay the safety of Plymouth Sound, but the killer gale was blowing diagonally across the entrance. Not enough to make the passage impossible; just enough to tempt the captains to try it. Some – the wiser ones as it turned out – anchored about a mile offshore between the Rame Head and Penlee Point. Now rain came on the wind and every now and then squalls would blot out the land. The light was fading and soon it would be dark.

Ride it out or run for it? That was the question. About 20 ships decided to anchor and ride it out, but the *Northumberland* decided to have a go. She was lucky. She made it only to go ashore in the Hamoaze, the principal anchorage for Navy ships for generations.

Next came the *Harwich*. She didn't get that far. She got into the Sound, but only just and went ashore on the rocks near Maker Point before she could reach the Hamoaze. She was a total loss.

Then the *Royal Oak* made her run for it. She too got into the Sound, but ran on shore almost gently "under Mount Edgecumbe House" and was towed off later.

The greatest tragedy was reserved for last. Now it was Skelton's turn. Under reefed topsails, *Coronation* drove for safety with the wind right behind her. Then either a gust caught her or the wind increased. She looked as though she was going to capsize for the battering of the seas had started a leak down below. Skelton knew his danger and acted at once. Orders were trumpeted into the gale and the carpenters sprang to their task. Within moments the great masts toppled down – they didn't need cutting right through before they snapped under their own weight. Skelton was too late. For a moment she was seen with just her ensign staff standing and then she rolled over and was gone. And gone with her was Skelton and most of his crew. Gone too was Colonel Laston and the detachment of Marines who were also aboard.

There is some suggestion that Skelton tried dropping his anchors at the last moment and that is when she was seen mastless and with just her ensign flying. There is some suggestion too that *Coronation* was not carrying a full crew at the time of the disaster, so how many were lost it is impossible to say. But that only 22 were saved we know by reading a letter dated the next day from Henry Greenhill, the Port Agent of Plymouth for the Commissioners of the Admiralty.

Greenhill seems a mean, ingratiating man, for this is what he wrote – and he didn't even start off his letter with the loss of *Coronation* and all those hundreds of men:

> "May It Please Your Honours,
>   I have received yours of the 1st instant and shall furnish Captain Evans with what Stores shall be needful

for his Ship, if they are in Stores or can be procured and am glad that you are satisfied of the injustice of his late complaints. I have written Mss. Lowes of Bideford whom I employed to hire the vessel for Kinsale to send me a Certificate of the Agreement, which shall be transmitted to you in Order to you making out a Bill for the same.

"Yesterday our Fleete was forced into this Harbour by a Violent Storme of wind att S: S: East, the *Coronation* was unfortunately lost between the Rame Head and Pen Lee Point having first cut all her Masts by ye Board, most of the third rate made for the Hammoze where about Three or Four of them went ashore and the Harwich oversett, but the rest are or will all gett off Shore with little damage.

"The Admiral hath directed me to supply such Ships as have received Damage with what is of absolute necessity for enabling them to go up this River, which we are now about and shall use the best husbandry possible and be as spareing as we can, though I fear this unhappy disaster will draw from Us a considerable quantity of Stores.

"It is now reported that the *Sovereign* and the *Dutchesse* are come into the Sound, who before were missing, and several other English and most of the Dutch ships have as yett no notice of, and suppose they did not beare away with the Fleete, but there is a rumour of their being in Torbay, God grant itt may prove true.

"I beg your pardon for not giving you this Account by Express sent Last night to the Admiralty, having been on board the *Elizabeth* and other Ships all ye afternoone in wind and raine till late att night and greatly fatigued.

　　　　　　　　"Your honoured and most humble Servant
　　　　　　　　　　　　　　　Henry Greenhill
Plymouth ye 4th September
1691

"There was about 22 of ye Seamen belonging to ye *Coronation* saved in their longboat and drove ashore upon some of ye Wreck, the Capn and Coll. Laston both drownd".

And that, as far as Henry Greenhill was concerned, appeared to be that. But the Admiralty had yet to close its books on the *Coronation*. The court-martial into the wreck throws little more light on the matter. It was held on board the *Dutchess* in the River Medway on Thursday, October 22nd, 1691.

President of the court-martial was Sir John Ashby, Vice-Admiral of the Red, and his fellow judges in the great stern cabin were Captains Jones, Nevill, Lestock, Bokenham, Gother, Hoskins, Edwards, Waters and Baker.

First matter to be dealt with was the loss of the *Harwich* and after hearing the facts the court "did discharge and acquit Captain Henry Robinson and all the rest of ye Officers belonging to ye same".

Then came the case of Skelton and the *Coronation*. In careful copperplate the clerk recorded:

"Also enquiry was made concerning the losse of their Majesties late ship ye *Coronation*, which was oversett off ye Ramhead on ye Coast of Cornwall. Resolved, that the opinion of ye Court is, that by a Butt-head starting, or some Planke giving way Shee sprung a Leake, and thereby was lost. And doe not find that there was any Neglect or failure of Duty in Captain Skelton, late Commander of ye sd Ship ye *Coronation*, or any of the officers belonging to ye same.

"Allso itt appears to ye Court that Mr. William Passinger Lately 1st Lieutenant of Ye *Coronation*, was absent from ye sd Ship by his Captain's Order, being sent to Falmouth for water and fresh provisions, and therfore the Court does discharge and acquit the sd Mr. Passinger, as to what relates to ye losse of ye Ship *Coronation*".

No more explanation of Passinger's strange trip. No more explanation about the loss of *Coronation*. No mention of any salvage of her great cannon. Well, they couldn't could they because she had gone down in deep water off Rame Head?

Well, no she hadn't. Her cannon were in fact in just a few feet of water off the tip of Penlee Point, but as no one knew that, the case of *Coronation* was well and truly closed. She and Skelton were forgotten for precisely 276 years.

In 1967, some local British Sub-Aqua Club amateur divers were enjoying a dive in the clear waters off Penlee Point. As they explored the seabed suddenly one of them noticed some encrusted cannonballs. Then more. And more. He followed a trail which led him into the kelp-covered rocks of Lady Cove. And there, to his amazement, pointing in all directions were nearly 20 ancient cannon. He and his partners parted the kelp and stared straight into the maws of even more. Piled beside them as though ready for firing were more heaps of cannonballs. In the end the divers counted 50 cannon on the seabed within a few feet of the shore and in only 20 feet of water.

Research showed that the only wreck big enough to have carried all those cannon and of approximately the right date for the types of guns was *Coronation*. But was it her? Another clue which strongly suggested that it was indeed *Coronation* was the discovery of giant bronze pulley wheels, probably from the steering gear of the ancient ship. Each was clearly marked with the Royal Navy's broad-arrow showing that it was Government property.

But they still couldn't prove it was Skelton's ship. Archaeologist-divers searched and searched but could not find one item that would positively say "Here lies *Coronation*". Arguments raged fiercely. "How can it be *Coronation?*" asked one side, "when she was seen to go down off Rame Head further along the coast". "She can't be any other ship", said others just as firmly, "where else could all those cannon have come from?" "Ah", came the reply, "the cannon – why didn't they salvage those valuable cannon? After all they are in such shallow water that anyone could duck-dive down to them!"

That last point was a good one. Even in the 17th century divers could work from a primitive diving bell at considerable depths and it is true that cannon were not just left if there was any chance of recovery. In 1977, however, there was a startling new development.

Peter McBride, a well-known diver-archaeologist, having searched all around Rame Head with metal-detecting instruments towed from a boat, finally got a strong reading only half-a-mile from Penlee Point in 60 feet of water. He dived and discovered at least 17 cannon and, most important of all, recovered a large pewter plate.

That plate when cleaned revealed the personal crest of Captain Charles Skelton. There was no doubt that McBride had found *Coronation*, complete with three large anchors. But where did that leave all those cannon closer in to the shore at Lady Cove on Penlee Point?

Despite all the arguments there is little doubt that those cannon are from *Coronation* and here, I think, is what really happened. In the surviving log-books of the ships which saw the sinking, there is an incredible variation of her position, ranging from the *Windsor Castle's* "oversett three miles from shore" to the *Ossory's* "saw the wreck on shore". Both are right.

When *Coronation* "oversett" she either broke up and dumped part of herself on McBride's site, or the bow section broke away – remember she was leaking – together with the anchors, some deck guns, and the contents of the galley, including Skelton's pewter plate, and this finally ended up where McBride found it. The rest of the capsized ship then drifted in to break up on the rocks of Penlee Point.

And the explanation of the failure to salvage any of those inshore cannon is simply because no one saw her final end. Remember the day was drawing to a close. In the huge seas of that storm, she was washed upside down with little showing except every now and then perhaps the dark line of her keel all the way from somewhere more towards Rame Head to Penlee Point. Perhaps darkness fell and covered her final impact with the shore. No one would be out on a night like that at the very tip of Penlee Point to see it. Came the dawn and all that could be seen around Lady Cove was the same sort of wooden wreckage which was strewn on the rocks of many other coves in the area.

Diving is still going on in the area of Lady Cove and when you walk out to that site, you may well see a diving boat and divers at work only a few feet from your vantage point. They are still hoping to find some positive evidence inshore – the final proof that *Coronation* is in two parts.

How to get there

Park the car in the large free car park at Cawsand. Leave by the car entrance, unless you fancy a pint of draught cider at the Smugglers Inn in Cawsand's little square – in that case leave the car park at the foot and make your way through the narrow streets towards the tiny beach.

Once out of the car entrance of the car park turn left and left again. Now across on your right you will see a lane leading up a hill and marked "Access Only". Walk up this lane and it will lead you for a mile through thick woodland to Penlee Point and the grave of *Coronation*. Through gaps in the trees on your left you will at first be able to look across Cawsand Bay to the old Napoleonic Fort on Picklecombe Point, which has now been converted into splendid flats.

Carry on down the lane – which is well-maintained for Ministry of Defence and Trinity House personnel who man the various establishments tucked into the coves below you on the left. (Please don't bring your car; there is nowhere to park it, though it does look tempting!)

After several hundred yards of this woodland walk – it is a public footpath – the road forks. Do not take the one leading down to the sea – it leads to a Ministry of Defence area – but stay on the top road. This curves to follow the rocks of the coast and in summer gives you some very Mediterranean-like views looking down on the clear water in the rocky inlets. After a mile you suddenly emerge from the trees and are almost on Penlee Point itself, all grey-slate rocks and gorse-studded turf. Here some thoughtful character has installed three wooden benches, which are perfect for our wreck-spotting.

Immediately to the left of these benches is what looks like a very ancient grotto set into the hillside. It is, however, not all that old, being built in Victoria's reign, a part of the great enthusiasm for follies in those times. In this case the enthusiasm came from one of the Earls of Mount Edgecumbe at nearby Mount Edgecumbe House.

Under the grotto is the remains of a World War Two gun

emplacement – this was a large gunsite during that war as can be seen by the remains of a small supply port on the northern side of the Point. On the Point itself is a very conspicuous white building with a large aerial and cones projecting from its roof. This is in fact a new electronic foghorn which pings rather than hoots its warning.

Look along the coast, round to the right from the Point, and the first rocky islet you see almost directly in front of the three seats is the marker for Lady Cove and it is just there that the guns of *Coronation* lie. If you were to swim down the gully on the left of the islet you would swim over some of them. When diving is taking place on the site, the seats provide a grandstand view of the diving boats and divers at work.

Incidentally, if you want to see some of the items recovered from the site by the amateur divers, you must go to Fort Bovisand, which lies across Plymouth Sound in Devon on the coast behind the far end of the Breakwater as you look out from Penlee Point.

Commander Alan Bax at the Fort will be delighted to show you the great bronze steering wheels of the ancient ship. It is best to telephone him first (0752-42570) so that he can arrange for you to look over the Fort as well during your visit. You can park right down by the entrance to the Fort after a scenic drive along the cliff-tops from Plymouth via Turnchapel to Staddon Heights before dropping down to Fort Bovisand. This is Britain's largest underwater centre, training divers for the North Sea oil rigs as well as teaching pleasure-diving amateurs about such things as underwater archaeology. Indeed, a team based on Fort Bovisand are leading the underwater hunt for final proof that all those guns on Penlee Point are from *Coronation*.

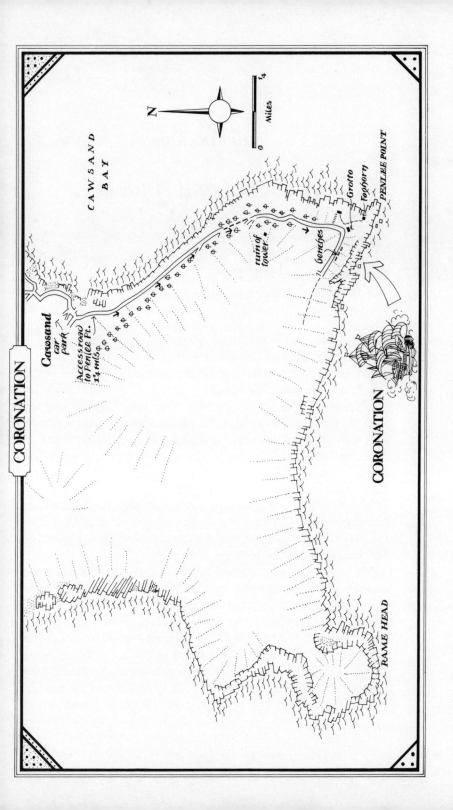

CHAPTER TEN

Mohegan and Andola

The date: October 14th, 1898.
The weather: fine with a south-east wind increasing steadily.

A brand-new passenger liner is on collision course with the Lizard peninsula of Cornwall. One hundred and six people are to die in the icy waters around the Manacles Reef when the ship hits the rocks at full speed.

The story of the *s.s. Mohegan* is quite amazing, because her suicide course had been set early on her run down the Channel and was never altered. Her course for disaster was passed on from helmsman to helmsman, watch after watch, without any question – even when she passed much too close to the Eddystone Lighthouse off Plymouth.

The *Mohegan* was a new ship. A luxury ship in which all her passengers travelled first class. She had been launched at Hull that very same year and was the largest ship built by Earle's Shipbuilding and Engineering Company.

She was originally ordered by the Wilson Line of Hull and was designed to run between London and New York. At the launching ceremony, complete with the obligatory bottle of champagne, however, the name that had the whole yard cheering was not *Mohegan*, but *Cleopatra* – 8,500 tons, 482 feet long, 52 feet in breadth and 34 feet 6 inches deep. Whether the Wilson Line was tired of waiting for the ship – she should have been completed the previous year, but was delayed for months by an engineers' strike – or whether they thought it best to snap

11   The end for the *Mohegan*

12   *Andola* aground on the Shark's Fin

up a quick profit, no one now knows, but they sold her as soon as the final licks of paint were dry.

Her new owners were the Atlantic Transport Company and they paid £140,000 for her. Her maiden voyage, as *Cleopatra*, was from Hull to London and then on to New York in July. Right from the start, the ship gave trouble. In insuring the ship the Atlantic Transport Line took £38,000 of the risk themselves and Lloyds carried the other £102,000. Perhaps they might not have taken so much of the risk on themselves if they had insured her after that first trip to New York.

For the new owners found out quickly that their investment was not all plain sailing. Despite her very modern layout and the fact that she was fitted with "steam steering engines and hand steering gear" and despite the fact that the Board of Trade had examined her carefully before passing her, her first voyage – with some of the owners on board – caused no end of bother.

The *Cleopatra* was temperamental. She gave a great deal of trouble with both her engines and boilers and her "quick trip home" from New York lengthened into 21 days at sea. The directors who were on that trip made sure that matters were put to rights and quickly. The ship was overhauled, her compasses were adjusted, she was inspected once more by the Board of Trade, and then she was ready for the New York trip once again. But first they renamed her. Now she was the *Mohegan* – a Red Indian word meaning "good canoe man". The new name was painted on all the lifebelts, and on the lifeboats, and on each side of the ship's bow in individual brass letters, each 14 inches high.

The only thing they didn't have time to rename was the ship's bell, which still bore the name of *Cleopatra* when she left Gravesend on Thursday, October 13th, 1898 for her second and last voyage. Those of her 53 first-class passengers who survived were to say later that they didn't like the idea of sailing on the 13th, but apparently none of them mentioned it at the time.

Her crew of 97 and six cattlemen on board had no time for such superstitious thoughts, for Captain R. Griffiths was a

Merionethshire man, who didn't like to see his crew idle. He was the commodore of the Atlantic Transport Line and was greatly experienced. In fact this was his third big steamship command.

A stiff breeze met the *Mohegan* as she came out into the Channel. The wind, veering between south-east and east, had more than a hint of winter in it, and passengers who were trying out their sea-legs wrapped up well. The ship had 1280 tons of general cargo – rice, tin, coffee, cheese, preserves, pitch, prunes, even church ornaments – in her holds.

In addition to that weight, she carried 1050 tons of bunker coal and had taken on 1180 tons of water ballast. The ship was trimmed well and the passengers found her motion not uncomfortable and their confidence in the ship rose even higher. What more could they ask? The food was good, the crew seemed efficient and polite, the Captain looked, indeed was, a man of great experience, and, if the worst came to the worst, look at those eight large steel lifeboats which, said the plaques at the lifeboat stations, could carry 234 people between them! Those passengers who were not seasick, settled down to enjoy a most pleasant voyage.

The next day the *Mohegan* was well on her way. The only untoward thing, which passed unnoticed by everyone except Engineer Officer Ferguson who was in charge of the *Mohegan's* engines, was that the lifeboat stations were not allocated. This was normally done in the company's ships on the second day out. This time it wasn't, and Ferguson, with his ten years of experience with the company, noticed it. Not that he worried about it. He had enough to do nursing his precious engines.

At ten o'clock in the morning Quartermaster Juddery took over the wheel. "West-three-quarters-north," said the man he relieved, and the watching officer made no comment. Having an officer present each time the wheel was handed over was a check that the correct course was being handed on. So west-three-quarters-north it was and Juddery found his spell at the wheel quite pleasant. The weather was fine, and the ship was well within sight of land. The Isle of Wight dropped back and Portland started to come up. The *Mohegan* was making an easy 14 knots and the ebb tide was with her. As the ship drew level with Portland Bill, Juddery handed over the wheel. It was exactly noon.

As he went below Juddery put out a steadying hand to one of the women passengers who was caught off balance by a sudden motion of the ship. She was, he thought, a fine-looking woman, but probably recovering from some illness and taking the voyage to put some colour back into her cheeks. He based this final observation on the looks of the man with the woman, Mrs Compton Swift. The man looked like a doctor. Juddery was right. The man was Mrs Swift's physician, Dr Fallows.

Luncheon was served in the saloon and, by all accounts, was an excellent meal. More of the sea-sick passengers were about now and the voyage seemed well settled in. In fact, "All well" was the signal passed by *Mohegan* to Prawle Point Coastguard at 2.50 p.m.

Quartermaster Butt took the wheel from 4 p.m. to 6. "West-by-north" was the course he was given by Quartermaster Blake and, as there was no word of interruption from Chief Officer Llewelyn Couch, that was the course Butt steered. And only a minute or two after he took the wheel the Eddystone Lighthouse was sighted at an angle of 45 degrees to the ship's course. At that moment, Juddery, who had been resting on his bunk after lunch, came up for a breath of air. As he came on deck he saw the Lighthouse at once. "She's close," he thought to himself, and mentally put the lighthouse only three miles from the starboard bow. Seeing him apparently unemployed, Chief Officer Couch interrupted Juddery's ponderings and ordered him to help with observations and entries in the log. Juddery noted carefully that the calculations showed the Eddystone to be passed at a little less than three miles and their speed to be eleven knots.

Mrs Compton Swift was another person who noted how close the ship was to the Eddystone. In fact she commented to Dr Fallows that the ship had been very close in most of the way down the Channel. Not many of the other passengers cared, though a young American singer, Miss Rodenbusch, going home with her step-mother, thought it a fine sight. The thoughts of most people were turning towards dinner. George Maule, the leader of the six cattlemen in the ship's company, had little to do except think about the next meal. His job was the care of the horses which the Line brought regularly to England from America for sale. His job would only start in earnest when the horses were loaded in New York. Until then he was determined to eat well and get as much rest as possible. Now, he decided, was the time for a nice cup of tea ...

Quartermaster Butt held firmly to the course which he had been given. The wind was freshening and blowing much more strongly from the south-east. Chief Officer Couch kept looking at the binnacle, and Butt was determined not to be caught off course for one second. He'd show Couch how a real quartermaster should steer!

He was concentrating so hard on this that when, at 5 p.m., Captain Griffiths appeared suddenly from behind him Butt almost jumped. The Captain stared at the course in silence. But soon, to Butt's relief, he moved away, apparently satisfied, and stood talking to Mr. Couch. At six o'clock, with a feeling of a job well done, Butt handed over the wheel to Quartermaster August in the presence of the Second Officer. "West-by-north", said Butt. "West-by-north it is," said Quartermaster August. The course for disaster was now confirmed. Only a new order could save the *Mohegan* from the Manacles. It never came.

As Butt handed over the wheel, Huntley in the crow's nest thankfully gave up his position to the ship's boy, Daniels. A little while later one of the deckhands, Seaman Wood, saw a light two points off the starboard bow. It was about three miles away and he thought it came from the shore. As he saw it, he heard the warning bell from the crow's nest. What the boy Daniels said, he could not make out, but he heard the reply from the bridge clearly enough. "All right" the voice said.

At 6.30 they started serving dinner in the saloon. Miss Rodenbusch and her step-mother, Mrs Grandin, were among the first to take their places. Mrs Compton Swift was rearranging her dress in her cabin, and Dr Fallows was waiting patiently outside to take her to dinner. He noted that the ship was much more lively now and put it down to the increased wind and sea. They were going to be late for dinner if Mrs Swift didn't hurry up. It was all very well attending your patient on a voyage, and Mrs Swift was paying him well, but dinner was dinner.

In the dining saloon, Mr Pemberton looked round the table at his wife, his two children and the nursemaid and made a mental note to see that the children had something in their cabin in future. By the time the meal was over they would be nearly asleep. At a nearby table, Mr John Hyslop, the measurer for the New York Yacht Club, started on his soup. Miss Katharine Noble, seeing that no one was waiting for her to start, decided to eat her soup anyway.

The minutes to disaster were ticking away. But still the *Mohegan* continued on her disastrous course. By now she had been seen from the shore. Rockets were fired to warn her. Blue fire – an early type of flare – was let off to show the ship that she was heading straight for the shore. James Hill, the lifeboat coxswain, of Porthoustock village, near the Manacles, was standing at the door of his stable when he first spotted her. "She's coming right in," he yelled and started running to alert his crew and get to the lifeboat station on the shore. He estimated that she was only a quarter of a mile away, and still coming with all lights blazing – "just like a London street". But he didn't know then that this crazy ship was the *Mohegan*. He thought it was the Irish steamer from Falmouth. Nothing else – indeed no ship – should be in the position that the *Mohegan* was now.

At last the Captain, who had not been dining with his passengers, seemed to have realised his danger. The *Mohegan* turned slowly to port, but at the speed she was travelling she had no chance. Whether the Captain heard the Manacle Bell, put there in 1838 to warn ships of the rocks, or whether he saw the flares and rockets, we shall never know, but the *Mohegan* turned directly into one of the main groups of the Manacle Rocks. She would have done better to go straight on shore.

With 30 seconds to go to 6.50 p.m. the engines were signalled to stop. Half a minute later the *Mohegan* struck.

Miss Rodenbusch was just finishing the "soup and fish". Mrs Compton Swift was just about to sit down. Miss Noble had finally finished her soup. Mr Ferguson, the Engineer Officer who had noticed that no lifeboat stations had been allocated, got the "Stop" signal very suddenly. Quick as he was, the engines had barely stopped turning when he heard, rather than felt, the ship strike. There was a jolt and a scraping noise like a cable running out of a chain-locker. Then a bigger noise. Water spurted into the engine room through the engineers' store cupboard on the starboard side. Seconds later it was pouring in.

Ferguson yelled orders to open the valves on the boilers as the water began to rise rapidly, forcing everyone out on deck. As Ferguson reached the open air – he was the last out – the ship took a sudden list to port and all the electric lights went out as the sea reached the generators near the engine room.

We know now the explanation for the two shocks that the *Mohegan* suffered. The first one was when she hit the Manacle Rock called "The Vase", because her great steel rudder has been seen by divers still embedded in the rock today. Then the *Mohegan*, rudderless, careered on into the outer face of the main group called "The Voices" and there she finally came to rest. Her wreckage is there underwater today.

In the dining saloon the shocks of striking had been felt even more clearly. It hardly needed the steward, who hurried down stairs and shouted "All on deck to save yourselves", to tell them that things had gone terribly wrong. Most people made their way to the deck with little trouble as the lights did not go out until the last passengers were on the stairway.

Mrs Compton Swift and Dr Fallows once on deck soon became adjusted to the darkness and found it not so dense. In fact it was only just dark. Mrs Swift said to Dr Fallows: "We'll need lifebelts most." Dr Fallows went to get them and came back carrying in addition to the lifebelts, his coat and Mrs Swift's sealskin bag. By now Mrs Swift did not feel so frightened. The ship did not appear to her to be in great danger so she asked Dr Fallows if he had her jewel-case too. "No," said the Doctor, "but I can easily get it." "Don't worry about it," said Mrs. Swift, regretting having asked for it, but he had rushed off.

Minutes passed and Dr Fallows did not return. The deck tilted to port and now Mrs Swift was really frightened. She relied on the Doctor and so set off to find him. As she started down the stairs to the cabins, she found the Doctor coming up. At the foot of the steps he was waist-deep in water. The ship was filling rapidly, but together they managed to get up on deck again.

The list to port increased. So much so that the port lifeboats were in an almost impossible position. The Captain on the bridge shouted the traditional order – "Women and children first" as the seamen struggled with the first of the port lifeboats, but it swung inboard, owing to the list, and jammed. The seas around the ship were now looming up over the frightened passengers and the ship settled lower in the water. She was going fast. The seamen abandoned the jammed boat and moved to the second. This was successfully lowered into the water. Twenty-seven passengers were safely in, but there was no seaman aboard to take charge. However two seamen swam out to her and, after a struggle, they got in and within seconds the boat was swept from sight into the night.

It was now impossible to get the other port-side lifeboats away and Miss Noble, who had found a place in one of them, had to get out again. She heard the Captain cry: "Hurry up with the boats," and then order people over to the starboard side.

The position with the starboard lifeboats was not much better. However much the seamen struggled to get them clear, they couldn't be lowered. Miss Noble couldn't find a place in any of them, even though the Fourth Officer tried to help her. Finally, seeing that it was no use, he found her a place above the railing, where she should be able to swim clear when the water reached her. A steward gave her a lifebelt, and then Miss Noble sat there trying to keep calm while the ship sank under her.

Mrs Compton Swift had been more fortunate, or so she thought. She had found a place in one of the boats on the starboard side with 25 other passengers. She heard the Captain yelling at his crew: "Men! Aren't you men? Can't you launch those lifeboats?" and finally one boat was in the water. In it was Mrs Swift, Miss Rodenbusch, her stepmother Mrs Grandin and some children.

At this moment there was an explosion. The water had reached the boilers. The ship shuddered and Chief Officer Couch gave orders to cut free all the lifeboats so that they could float off when the ship went down. That time now seemed only seconds away.

It says a lot for Mrs Compton Swift that she still had her wits about her. Many of the passengers were fixed in terror, clinging to the railings. Others huddled together on any part of the ship which was still above the fast-advancing waves. Mrs Swift had spotted another danger. The lifeboat in which they were seated was still fastened by ropes to the ship at both ends and would be dragged under when the ship sank. She screamed to the man next to her in the bows to cut the rope. He did so and then started the knife on a perilous journey from hand to hand along the crowded boat to the man in the stern. Unfortunately, this man panicked, shouted that he couldn't cut through the rope, and dropped the knife. It fell into the bottom of the boat and there was no time to find it. A huge wave came out of the darkness and flicked the boat over as though it were a child's toy. Most of these in it were spilled out into the spume around the *Mohegan*.

On the bridge Captain Griffiths looked around in despair. His once fine ship was now a shambles. The screams and cries in the water told him that most of his crew and passengers were struggling in the cold Cornish sea. He had managed to get some rockets fired and, from others exploding in the sky not far away, he knew that help was coming. The trouble was that from the feel of the ship he knew that the *Mohegan* would not be there to meet her rescuers. The ship lurched again – deeper. He had one more command to give: "Get as many women as you can into the jigger rigging!" At least the water might not be too deep for the rigging to stay above the sea. The Captain took a firmer grip on the bridge-rail. He was going down with his ship. It was now four minutes past seven and the soup tureens chinkled together in the swirling water in the dining saloon. They, together with the rest of the plates for the meal that was never finished, slid out through the hole that the boiler explosion had blown in the side of the galley. The *Mohegan* was going ...

Mr John Hyslop, the yachtsman from New York, watched the Manacle Rocks start to rear up beside the ship. He knew that no more boats were going to get away. So he decided to take his chance in the mizzen rigging. He was only just in time. At exactly 7.15 p.m. the *Mohegan* settled stern first. The waves overtook Hyslop in his climb, but he struggled on up, fearing every second that he would become entangled and drown. Finally, however, he broke free of the water and found the Assistant Stewardess, Quartermaster Juddery, and another seaman close to his perch. Hyslop shifted from one foot to another to ease the strain. Over and over again in the darkness he pictured the last moment of the *Mohegan* - and saw Chief Officer Couch dive cleanly away from the stern just as the water closed over it.

George Maule, the chief stockman, thought at first that the *Mohegan* had collided with another ship. He rushed up on deck and ran straight into Couch and teamed up with him. Couch shouted: "Keep cool, boys, and we'll get the ladies and children off first". Then he and Maule made sure that every woman and child had a lifebelt. Maule stuck with Couch to the end and, when finally Couch dived away, Maule jumped over after him.

William Ferguson, the Engineer Officer, who had injured his left hand badly in efforts to launch the lifeboats, was one of many who were flung into the water when the ship gave her final lurch. After swimming for nearly an hour he found himself bumping against the ship's funnel which, together with the masts, seemed to be the only parts of the ship above water. He climbed up on to the funnel. The screams and cries in the water below him soon died away as the strong seas pounded on to the nearby rocks.

Katharine Noble found herself in the water very suddenly.

She swam to a plank and drifted with it. Then a larger piece of wreckage floated by and she changed over to that.

Mrs Compton Swift found herself in darkness, utter and complete. She thought she had been drawn down under the *Mohegan*. She was quite conscious. A body bumped against her and it cried out in a child's voice. Mrs Swift tried to hold the little body up, but it drifted from her.

Then a man's voice said something unintelligible in the darkness. When Mrs Swift answered, there was no reply. Only gradually did it dawn on Mrs Swift that she was underneath an upturned lifeboat. She struggled desperately to get free, but found herself to be trapped fast by her foot. Somebody else was there too. Another body bumped into her and Mrs Swift struggled to hold that up above the water. After what seemed a long, long time, the woman she was holding started to scream – and scream. Mrs Swift found herself thinking quite calmly that the voice which went on screaming was a trained one – she was right; it was Miss Rodenbusch – and said to herself, "That's good, that sort of voice will save us because it will carry well."

By 7.20 p.m. James Hill, the coxswain of the Porthoustock lifeboat, had got his boat launched and was heading for the Manacles. He burnt a white light, but received no reply. The wind was freshening even more and the sea rising. Suddenly they spotted a ship's lifeboat upside down. From underneath it came the sound of a woman screaming.

When the lifeboatmen managed to right the steel hull, there was no doubt that Miss Rodenbusch was alive, but, looking at the other figure with its leg jammed between the seat and the side of the boat, one of the lifeboatmen said, "It's no good taking this one, she's dead". Mrs Compton Swift heard the words with horror. "I'm not dead!" she shrieked. "I'm not dead! You must save me!" To get her free lifeboatman Francis Trip climbed into the ship's boat and with an axe chopped the wooden seat away. Finally Mrs Swift, bruised and battered, lay beside Miss Rodenbusch in the bottom of the lifeboat, out of the way of the oars, as the lifeboatmen resumed their search for survivors.

Within minutes the Porthoustock boat found the one *Mohe-gan* lifeboat which had got away. Among others on board were Mr Pemberton, his wife, two children and their maid. James Hill burned three white flares to show he needed help and returned to shore with the survivors. Then he set out again for the wreck. Coming up as close as he dared, he heard cries from the rigging.

Quartermaster Juddery timed his dive from the rigging just right. Along the line he carried to the lifeboat followed Mr Hyslop and all those who had taken refuge with him.

Lifeboats from all along the coast were now arriving. George Maule was picked up by the Falmouth boat after seven hours in the water. Engineer Ferguson was taken off the funnel. Miss Noble was found on her piece of wreckage after floating about for hours.

But 106 were drowned, their bodies littering the nearby beaches. Many were buried in a mass grave in St Keverne Churchyard, near tablets marking earlier disasters on the Manacles.

The Board of Trade inquiry opened, and during most of it the red funnel and masts of the *Mohegan* stayed above water, marking the Manacles more clearly than any buoy or bell. The work of salvage started and went on. The inquiry in London dragged on too, checking whether the *Mohegan's* compasses had been properly adjusted, or whether some other reason could be found for her suicide course.

The inquiry was hampered by the fact that practically every officer who could tell them the answers – including the Captain – was dead. Finally on November 26, the inquiry closed with the verdict that "the cause of the stranding of the vessel was that a wrong course was steered of west-by-north after the vessel left the Eddystone". But the inquiry failed to find out why such a course was steered. It was left like that. The court warmly commended Hill of the Porthoustock lifeboat and Engineer Juddery for their bravery. And, as though waiting for the verdict, soon afterwards the *Mohegan* slid off the rocks and was gone down into the deep. You can however see the rocks which killed her, rise each low tide out of the sea, just as menacing and dangerous today as they were all those years ago.

How to get there

First of all, we need to reach the little village square of St Keverne. St Keverne is approached either from Falmouth or Helston using the B3293 across the bleak Goonhilly Downs. On your right you will pass the great satellite tracking dishes of British Telecom's "Goonhilly Downs Earth Station" before driving into more sheltered countryside leading to St Keverne.

St Keverne Church is set back on your left as you enter the village, its entrance almost squeezed in between the shops and the two pubs in the square! The church is mainly 15th century, though the tower fell down and was rebuilt in 1770. It is from this church that the Manacles probably take their name, not, as most people believe, from the idea that once on the reef you never get off. "Maen eglos" is the old Cornish for "stone church" or "church rocks", probably a reference to the fact that from the Manacles you can see the church. It is a corruption of this old Cornish which gives us "Manacles".

In the churchyard you will find the simple great cross which marks the mass grave of the *Mohegan* victims. It bears the single word "*Mohegan*". In the churchyard too, more graves mark the last resting place of other victims from other ships. In the church itself tablets are to be seen in memory of even more casualties of the Manacles.

You now have to decide whether to park in the square and walk the mile or so down to the spot near Porthoustock where you can see the site of the wreck (it is steep even by road), or whether to take the easy route by car. Either way follow the signposts for "Porthoustock".

At Porthoustock you will find yourself looking out to sea

across a grey shingle beach – the car can be parked at the back near the old lifeboat house from which James Hill set out on his rescue mission. The beach of grey stones at Porthoustock is flanked on each side by quarry buildings projecting into the sea like cliffs. It was from the chutes on these buildings that the coasters carrying the quarried stone were loaded as they tied up alongside. The quarries on both sides are now disused. On your right is Manacle Point.

From Porthoustock it is easy to walk up to the top of Manacle Point. Once on the top look out to sea to the south-east and you will see the great red Manacle Buoy. This marks the limit of the danger from the Manacles themselves and its bell warns off shipping which ventures too close. The Manacles cover about one-and-a-half square miles, many of the rocks being hidden just out of sight, particularly at high tide. Just inside that bell, you will see, at low tide, the dark rocks which the *Mohegan* struck. Nearby you may well see a diving boat anchored in position, for skin-divers are still discovering poignant items amid the tangled wreckage of the ship on the seabed below. One recent discovery was a brass case containing a hypodermic syringe in perfect condition and I like to think that this belonged to Dr Fallows, the doctor in attendance upon Mrs Compton Swift. He was drowned and his body was washed up further down the coast.

Before leaving Manacle Point, look down and you will see the grave of yet another ship. That great razor-backed jagged rock just off shore is called "Shark's Fin".

The "Shark's Fin" rock caused the end of the sailing ship pictured, wrecked, on the cover of this book – the *Andola*. She was a 2,093-ton full-rigged steel sailing ship, homeward bound with a cargo of grain from Seattle to Falmouth. Despite encountering gale after gale, and taking 180 days – six months! – over it, she finally reached Falmouth on January 29th, 1895. She took on fresh water and food, but on the same day an order came from her owners that she was to sail at once for Hull to discharge her cargo. Harsh as it was, orders were orders in those days, and she sailed on the evening tide. Out she went – into more high winds. This time she had to tack right

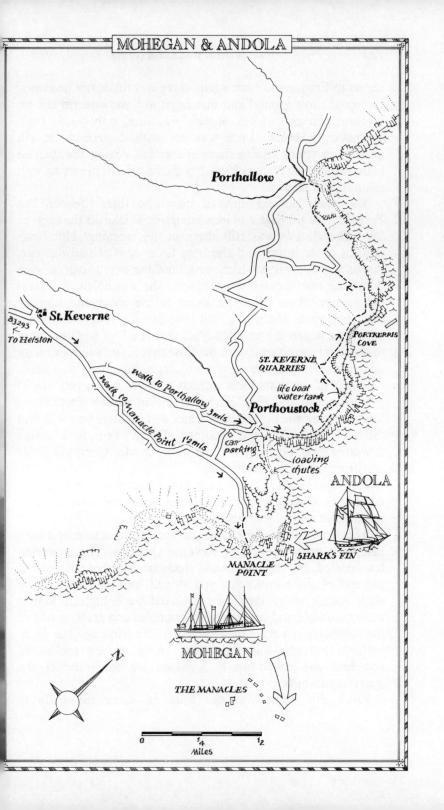

MOHEGAN & ANDOLA

Porthallow

St. Keverne

B3293
To Helston

PORTKERRIS COVE

ST. KEVERNE
QUARRIES

Walk to Porthallow 3 mls

Walk to Manacle Point 1½ mls

life boat
water tank

Porthoustock

car
parking

loading
chutes

ANDOLA

SHARK'S FIN

**MANACLE
POINT**

MOHEGAN

THE MANACLES

N

0   ¼   ½
Miles

across to France and back again to try and make any headway. In fact she lost ground and that night in a snow-storm she hit the northern end of the Shark's Fin rock, only yards from Porthoustock beach. Luck was not with the *Andola* at all, because in trying to fire flares sparks fell among the distress maroons and explosions blew her deckhouse to pieces as well as injuring a seaman.

The crew put the injured man into their lifeboat, but Porthoustock lifeboat was soon alongside to take off the crew of 29. The *Andola* was still there in the morning. Her bows pointed to the south and she bore little signs of real damage, but in fact the waves which were breaking over the deck were doing the real damage down below. She was holed in several places, her wheat cargo expanded in the water and literally burst her open. She was a total loss. She lies today – or rather the plates which are practically all that is left of her lie – close to shore by the Shark's Fin. So close that if you swim out with just a mask on you can see the wreckage, though if you want to see some of the brass letters which bore her name, you should pay a visit to the Five Pilchards Inn at nearby Porthallow. There among the other wreck relics and pictures you will find them. Incidentally, the landlord, David Trip is a direct descendant of the Francis Trip who cut Mrs Compton Swift free from the *Mohegan* lifeboat.

Now that we have come back to the matter of the *Mohegan*, another short walk from Porthoustock Beach will enable you to see another relic of that disaster.

This time we leave the beach on the left hand side by a path that leads up to the old St Keverne Quarries. The quarrying has finished, but many huts and sheds are still there. Almost at the end of these buildings, you should turn and walk to the bank against which they are built. And there, high up almost unrecognisable and covered with brambles and grass, is one of the *Mohegan's* steel lifeboats. After the sinking, the boat, battered but still-watertight, was found on the rocks and somehow she ended up as a water-tank for some of the quarrymen's huts.

From this point you can walk on along the cliffs to

Porthkerris Cove and by a lane from there back to Porthoustock. It is quicker however to return the way you came. Porthkerris is the place from which the Ministry of Defence operates a torpedo testing range. Sometimes you can stand on the cliffs and watch torpedos being dropped into the sea from aircraft. But if these modern excitements are not present, the area around St Keverne and the rest of the Lizard does provide some of most dramatic cliff and shore scenery in the country.

CHAPTER ELEVEN

Anson

The date: December 29th, 1807.
The weather: blinding sleet on a south-westerly gale.

One hundred and twenty men of the Royal Navy were about to die in the foam on Loe Bar, near Porthleven in Cornwall, when the frigate *Anson* was deliberately run ashore.

Nelson's victory at Trafalgar had crushed the French and the main threat from their fleets, but two years later the Navy could not afford to relax. They still had to patrol the Channel to ensure that Britain's lifelines were kept open and free from any attacks on friendly shipping.

So the Channel patrols went on all through the winter of 1807 blockading the French ports. Fortunately the winter up until Christmas had remained mild and the work of the blockade was not arduous, though it did require a large number of ships to make sure it remained effective.

One of those ships was the *Anson*. Her job was to patrol the area around Brest and though the sailors on most of the other ships involved considered the weather mild, the crew of the *Anson* thought it distinctly chilly. They had not long been back from the West Indies, where the *Anson* had helped capture Coracoa Island, and the *Anson's* captain, Charles Lydiard, had been mentioned in dispatches for his brave conduct while commanding his sailors and marines in the shore fighting.

Some of the men still carried the suntan they had collected during those sweltering days, and looked distinctly odd under

124

13   The *Anson* wreck site and memorial

14   A 32-pounder cannon dragged from the sea by Naval
      divers on the *Anson* wreck

the leaden skies of Cornwall. The *Anson*, too, did not take kindly to the Cornish seas. She had never been a great sailer and belonged to an awkward class of ship, a 44-gun fifth-rate, though she had been cut down to a third-rate, and still carried massive 32-pounder guns. Where other frigates were creatures of great sailing ability, the *Anson*, like the rest of her class, wallowed along and had to be fought every inch of the way. That lack of mobility was to play a major part in her destruction.

On Christmas Eve, however, she was not required to move and scarcely bobbed at her moorings in Falmouth Harbour. Her crew thought themselves very fortunate to be in port over Christmas, though it was clear she would soon be rejoining the Brest squadron. Loading stores and water kept the crew busy enough, but not so busy that they didn't have time for gossiping. Gossip soon turned to rumour which passed quickly from man to man – the *Anson* was to be pay ship for other vessels still at sea.

It was a silly rumour. The Navy was not in the habit of paying men while at sea. There was nothing to spend it on except gambling or buying other men's tots of rum. And no captain would risk that sort of dissension during the tiresome sweeps of a blockade. Each and every captain firmly believed that "The Devil makes work for idle hands" and acted accordingly.

But though Captain Lydiard kept his men busy loading and preparing his ship for sea, he did nothing to deny the "pay-ship" rumour. It is, of course, unlikely that he knew of it. Captains rarely talked to crewmen, many of whom were victims of the press gangs. So each load of unidentified stores was indicated with a nod and a wink as the repository of "the pay". It is almost certain that this rumour was spread to the shore by the various lightermen who plied with provisions between ship and quay.

On Christmas morning Captain Lydiard called for his boat and went ashore. Once there he made his way first to the home of his friend, Commander Thomas Sulivan, and then the two men went on to "Woodlands", the house of a Captain James.

The men dined heartily, and Lydiard returned aboard late that night. Captain Lydiard was not alone. His friend, Commander Sulivan, had accepted, perhaps when the port was flowing free, an invitation to join *Anson* for a cruise as the Captain's guest. On board, the crew had been confined to ship, but slept heavily. Extra food and rum had made its appearance, as well as many a jar smuggled aboard by the lightermen.

But there was to be no long sleep for anyone. Soon after dawn on Boxing Day, *Anson* was towed out of Falmouth Roads by her own boats, and her last voyage had begun.

It was a dreary morning, cloudy and cheerless, and those of the crew and officers with thick heads felt worse when the boats were shipped and under her own sail the ship rounded the sheltering headland. Rain was in the air, and a freshening breeze from the south-west had a nip in it which made everyone keep a weather eye open for the icy drops of sea, which sprayed up and across the deck each time the bow of the *Anson* ploughed into the waves.

Lydiard put the *Anson* on a southerly tack almost as soon as she had left Falmouth in order to clear the feared Manacle Rocks as widely as possible. He knew only too well how many ships had come to grief because they had not given those half-hidden reefs a wide enough berth (see Chapter 10). And then he continued on this course to clear the Lizard too.

As the day wore on the *Anson* weaved tack by tack down the Channel, but all the time the weather was getting worse. Soon the *Anson* was in the middle of a violent storm with the wind strengthening to gale force and bringing with it sleet which made each ice particle sting any unprotected face. Though the coast near Ushant was sighted during a gap in the white cloud which now seemed to surround them, Captain Lydiard decided that it would be impossible to join the rest of the Fleet off Brest in such conditions. He turned back for Falmouth. And though the *Anson* was no great sailer, now she seemed to fly along before the wind.

In fact she went faster than any of her officers thought possible. In the clouds of sleet and spray they could only work out their position by something close to guesswork; no sights could be taken in such weather. On and on she ran before the gale until even those who knew her to be a slow ship became worried. In such conditions, any ship could be on the rocks before there would be time for anyone to shout a warning. Captain Lydiard knew that full well. He doubled his lookouts and reduced canvas until he only had enough up to give the helmsmen steerage.

Suddenly in the early evening of December 27th, the wind dropped. Not enough to halt the *Anson's* onward rush, but enough to drop the sleet and rain a little. And almost at once came the cry of "Land-ho!" from one of the lookouts. For a while in that lull the land could be seen by everyone on deck. A great dark towering mass some nine leagues off. It bore north-north-west by compass and the *Anson's* bows pointed directly at it. Captain Lydiard consulted quickly with Commander Sulivan, whose local knowledge left him in no doubt where they were. The dark cliffs ahead were those of the Lizard. *Anson* had returned almost to the spot from which she had set out. But there was one important deadly difference. They were in Mounts Bay and the Lizard now stood between them and the shelter of Falmouth.

In the circumstances it might have been called a great feat of navigation – to get them back so close to Falmouth relying only on the compass – but it was just that bit out to make the difference between life and death.

It was now, too, that the poor sailing qualities of the *Anson* were to contribute to her destruction. As the wind increased again from the south-west, Captain Lydiard tried to sail her out of trouble. He turned into the wind and tried to tack her out of the bay and away from the land. But no matter how hard he and the crew tried, she wouldn't do it. She couldn't. On each tack they lost a little more sea-room and now, caught on a lee shore, she was slowly, but surely being blown towards the foam which marked the land between Gunwalloe and Porthleven.

While they still tacked, Captain Lydiard consulted again with Commander Sulivan and this time asked his senior officers for suggestions. But they had no ready answers. The ship was, without doubt, embayed, and nothing they could do, even with all their collective experience of the sea, would get them out of it. Unless ... unless the wind slackened. But the wind showed no sign of doing that. If anything, it seemed to be increasing.

Captain Lydiard listened, heard nothing that gave him any comfort and then made the only choice open to him. Bringing the *Anson* head to wind, he ordered the anchors to be dropped.

Some people – there are always some who work from hindsight – said that he should have done this earlier. But who is to say that he was wrong to try and sail his ship out of trouble first? Certainly, his attempt at anchoring in such enormous seas was a desperate one, but for those on board it was the last resort. And it didn't go well.

Two anchors were dropped, but the seas were so great that first one and then the other cable parted. The drift towards the iron shore began again. Another anchor, the best bower, with a fresh cable, rousted out from the cable tier, was now put down to stay the ship. But such was the *Anson's* rate of drift, even under bare poles, that the entire cable was out in seconds. It was quickly made fast to the anchor bits so that a further length could be spliced on. It was now dark and the job was almost impossible. But somehow, with men clinging anywhere they could and soaked and battered by each successive wave, it was done. Once released again this new cable hissed out through the hawse-hole at such a rate that no one could check it. Finally its entire length was out and only then was the ship brought to, head to wind.

The cable holding the ship now extended like a steel rod, bar-tight, pointing back into the dark and the heart of the gale.

A ship moored in conditions much less severe than those the *Anson* now faced, would need some form of protection for its cable against the chafing and continual movement across the lip of the hawse-hole. Lieutenant Thomas Gill of the *Anson*, now watching the cable closely and anxiously, knew this very well, but serving or wrapping the cable with strips of canvas would mean raising the rope from the hole to enable the protecting canvas to be passed underneath it and so make a continuous parcel around it. He knew too that in these conditions they could never do it; the cable never seemed to go slack for a second.

For the moment the *Anson* did seem to be safe, but the ship's officers knew it could not last. Once again Captain Lydiard called them all together. Not to consult them this time, but to tell them what he proposed to do next. When the cable snapped. Not "if" but "when". When it snapped, he proposed to run the ship on shore. He would put up enough sail to give steerage way and then deliberately aim for the beach at Loe Bar. Commander Sulivan had told him of the long beach there, and his charts showed that there were no rocks on the run in. At least there were no rocks marked on the charts between the ship and that part of the shore.

Once the ship struck, it would be every man for himself. All were to be on deck and provided the bow was well embedded in the beach he hoped that most could leap to safety. The men were to be told of this plan, and all would come on deck when ordered, not before. And so they waited. Lieutenant Thomas Gill, seeing the way the cable bent over the hawse-hole and noting the little jerks of the strands of the cable at each wave, had expected the cable to part swiftly. But hour after hour passed and still it held.

It held so long in fact that the crew began to hope that perhaps it would hold until the wind went down. Certainly it held through the darkest hour before dawn but, just as the sky began to lighten sometime after 5 a.m., without warning, the cable was no longer there. For a few long moments, *Anson* was free and broadside to the wind, but then Captain Lydiard's shouted orders got enough sail up to make her manageable. Now she drove wildly towards the land, the helmsman aiming directly at the centre of the black mass with a white border that was the shore.

The off-watch men came swiftly on deck at the order and now as the light strengthened, those straining their eyes towards the shore realised that they were not alone. Lining the shore from Porthleven to Gunwalloe were thousands of waiting faces. News of a wreck travelled fast and not all those waiting thousands were there to render aid and assistance to shipwrecked mariners. Many came to see what they could salvage, and the devil take the poor sailor.

Now above the howl of the gale the *Anson* men and women – for in keeping with the Navy's custom at that time there was a few "wives" aboard – could hear a new sound. At first it was just a mutter, but then as the ship raced closer, it blossomed into a boom – the boom of surf on a windswept beach. Now the *Anson* almost planed in to her death, acting like some great surf-board in the grip of the giant rollers. At this stage in her headlong rush she remained remarkably steady. So much so that Captain Lydiard and Commander Sulivan found no difficulty in lashing themselves to the same stanchion which held the wheel. For a moment as the beach seemed only yards away, she wallowed in a trough and the wheel span helplessly between the two helmsmen. Then as the next sea towered high above her poop, she was hurled onward and for a heart-stopping second Lydiard thought he had done it and she would carry on right up the beach.

But it was not to be. Less than 100 feet from the actual shore, the *Anson* took the bottom, broached to, and ground to a stop broadside to the beach. Her high poop, crowded with men, gave a sinew-stretching lurch and many of those who had sought safety there in preparation for a quick dash along the ship and over the bow to the beach, were flung into the raging sea. They stood no chance at all, every one of them being choked to death by cold, sand-thick salt water.

Now the ship lay practically on her beam ends, with the wind-driven waves bursting high over her hull. But all was not lost. The main-mast had broken off short and lay like a causeway between ship and shore. As each wave lifted the ship, broke, and then washed back, the trunk of the mast disappeared, but each time it reappeared again through the froth. Sailors, accustomed to the difficulties of sail high among the rigging, made short work of such a perilous trip to shore. Some women made it too. As each wave passed a new group made a dash along the mast to safety. It was such a successful exit from the ship that even a woman whose thigh had been broken was carried along it.

Captain Lydiard and Commander Sulivan ignored the easy way out. They remained to the last, keeping themselves in position, still lashed to the wheel stanchion. As they looked about them to see that all who could leave had done so, Lydiard could see that his ship was breaking up beneath him. They watched helplessly as a young midshipman, the son of the ship's surgeon, called out to his father as he was lifted bodily by another wave and smashed down between two cannon on the gun-deck. It was clear that he had been killed instantly. His father, the surgeon, totally distraught, left his own place of safety under the shelter of the wheelhouse, and rushed to help the boy. As he did so, another wave roared over the ship. The solid wall of water threw the surgeon against the lee side with such force that he too never moved again.

Not all the watchers on shore were content to let the men of the *Anson* die. Not all were there just for what they could snatch. The local vicar and another local man risked their own lives in the enormous surf and swam out to the wreck with lines along which many sailors made their escape.

Now that there appeared to be only the two of them left alive on the ship, Lydiard urged Sulivan to take his chance along the mast. Together they dashed to the spot where the end of the mast should reappear among the foam. Held by the remains of the rigging, it was close to the stump of the mast. Just as the two men were about to jump for the mast and safety, Lydiard saw one of the ship's boys, rigid with fear and clinging to the stump of the mast. As Sulivan started on his way along the mast, the Captain turned back to the boy, and regardless of his own danger, spent several precious seconds trying to coax the lad into a dash for the beach. Those precious seconds were too expensive. The next wave broke. It foamed around the mast-stump and carried both the Captain and the boy over the side of the ship to their deaths.

It was a monster wave. Sulivan, seeing it begin, dropped across the mast and clung tight to the cordage. The water passed over him and as it receded he was able to complete the rest of the journey to the beach. He was only just in time. No ship could stand the battering the waves were now giving to the *Anson* and she began to break apart.

One hundred and forty men had survived and Lieutenant Gill, finding himself the only surviving officer of the ship, gathered them together, and moved them overland in stages back to Falmouth, where they quartered aboard the *Tromp*.

Behind them on the beach they left wholesale looting before soldiers moved in to protect the little that was left of what had been washed ashore. Aboard the *Tromp*, Lieutenant Gill sat down to write the dispatch to the Admiralty which he knew would mean his own court-martial, following the normal Naval practice of court-martialling the senior survivor of any shipwreck. It was not only a means of getting at the guilty, but also a neat and tidy way of inquiring into the cause of any loss.

So, on the morning of Tuesday, January 5th, 1808, the Captains who were to make up the court assembled on a great man o'war anchored at Plymouth in the Hamoaze. The court-martial flag was hoisted and the convening gun fired. And Lieutenant Thomas Gill of H.M.'s late ship, the *Anson*, was called forward to tell the court exactly what happened on the occasion of the ship running on shore near Porthleven, just over two miles from Helston, Cornwall.

Gill told his story straightforwardly, and in the still of the big cabin, the Captains listened. But they didn't only listen. From time to time they shot questions at the young Lieutenant.

"Why were the guns not put overboard to lighten ship?" Both the Lieutenant and the questioner knew the answer. It was an easy question to ask in the calm of an anchored ship in sheltered waters, but not one to be considered in the teeth of a gale and with a bucking deck wet with sea.

Without hesitation Gill answered that to cut a cannon loose in the confines of a gun deck in such weather would be suicidal. Such a weight of metal, once loose, would trundle from port to starboard and back again like a huge battering ram until it finally smashed its way clear through the side of the ship. To say nothing of the men who would be injured or killed in trying such a thing.

"Why were not the masts cut away to lessen the play of wind on the ship?"

Another easy question, and one to which Gill had an even better answer. No sailor likes to destroy his motive power and in this case as the court knew, without the mast very few would have survived at all. Gill went then straight on with his statement and when it was all taken down with the clerk's quill, he was allowed to retire. Finally the court had all the evidence it needed. They considered it. And in his final words the President of the court summed it all up like this:

"The court is of the opinion that the cause of the loss of His Majesty's late ship *Anson* was in consequence of her endeavouring to make land in a violent gale of wind and thick weather, and that the *Anson* was not prepared in a state of readiness to come to an anchor upon a lee shore in such tremendous weather as the ship had to encounter". Gill was cleared and the Admiralty files on *H.M.S. Anson* were closed.

But some good was to come from the wreck of the *Anson*. Among those watchers on the shore had been a man called Henry Trengrouse of Helston. He saw the sailors die in the sea only yards from safety and was so appalled at the disfigured and battered corpses strewn on the beach that he determined that such a thing should not happen again without those on shore being able to offer some effective means of rescue. He returned home to think of some device that could be used in the future. He came up with the musket-fired rocket lifeline, which was the fore-runner of the rocket apparatus which is still in use today, and which over the years following the *Anson* wreck was to save thousands of lives.

Meanwhile, following the discovery of several gold coins on Loe Bar, the story that the *Anson* was the pay-ship for the fleet spread once again. These coins, however, are more likely to be the contents of Captain Lydiard's own "purse" and "treasure wreck" stories can be discounted.

Some salvage work has been done on the *Anson*. In 1903 a cannon was raised. In 1961, Roland Morris, an ex-helmet diver and owner of the Admiral Benbow, restaurant and ship museum in Penzance, raised more, and in 1964, divers from

H.M.S. Seahawk, the Royal Navy helicopter station at nearby Culdrose, lifted others.

How to get there

From Porthleven, a large village centred around its fishing harbour, it looks tempting to walk along Porthleven Sands to the south. The sands run for two miles and at first are backed by low cliffs with houses, but after that the scenery inland gets wilder. One mile along the walker will get to Loe Bar and the site of the shipwreck. But be warned. The so-called "Sands" are not sand at all. They are made up of tiny grains of rounded stones. The locals call them "stone seeds". They may be pretty, but their real disadvantage as far as walking is concerned is that your feet sink in and any distance becomes a hard slog, though an alternative is a rough road along the cliffs.

A much better way to visit the *Anson* is to go from Helston, the market town of the Lizard, and that "quaint old Cornish town" of the Furry Dance, which is held on May 8th each year. From the town you take the Porthleven road and just outside the town, a sign says "Private path to Penrose". This is the way to Loe Bar itself. Please note it is a private path and no dogs are allowed. Note also that it closes at 6 p.m. in winter and 8 p.m. in summer. On Sundays it is often shut. It is, however, a beautiful walk, following the River Cober's valley, and in one mile you come to Loe Pool. This fresh-water lake is surrounded by woods and, like every other sizeable piece of water in Cornwall, is said to be the pool into which King Arthur's sword, Excalibur, was thrown!

In another mile you will reach Loe Bar itself. The Bar, too, has plenty of legends attached to it. In fact it is a 600-foot wide (at its narrowest) pile of flint shingle and runs for a quarter of a mile between the cliffs on either side. Behind this bar the water piles up to form the lake of Loe Pool. The *Anson* struck almost exactly beneath the centre of the Bar. If she had come in like that 800 years earlier, there may have been no shipwreck at all. In the 11th century Loe Bar did not exist and ships came right in from the sea and up to the tin-mining town of Helston. The *Anson* struck exactly where the deep water channel into the river would have been.

What caused the Bar? There is some evidence to suggest that it was thrown up by the sea in a matter of days. Certainly by 1302 it was there. In Henry VIII's time it was of considerable size and had to be cut through to lower the level of the water which was flooding the lower part of Helston.

One legend about the formation of the Bar says that the giant Tregeagle was condemned to move sand from one cove to another and whilst employed in this endless labour – the sea kept washing the sand back – he accidentally dropped a sack of sand at the mouth of the river thus forming the Bar in one instant.

Though the level of the water today is controlled by culverts, in the mid-19th century the Mayor of Helston still had to ask permission from the lord of the manor to "open the Bar" and handed over a leather purse containing three halfpence. A small trench was then cut in the Bar and the water rapidly enlarged it. An eye-witness to this operation then wrote this: "The spectacle is one of the grandest that can be imagined. The rush of the emancipated element, the conflux of the waves and the contents of the lake, and the numerous cascades and eddies, often glistening in the beams of the moon, altogether form a scene of singular wildness and beauty, whilst the roar of the troubled water lends its aid to impress the mind of the beholder". He then added somewhat sadly: "The bar thus removed for a time is in a few days thrown up as before".

This return of the Bar by the sea would seem to be the explanation for its creation. Certainly in January 1924, out of a comparatively calm sea came a "tidal wave" which did a lot of damage at Porthleven. It threw vast quantities of sand and shingle on to and over the Bar.

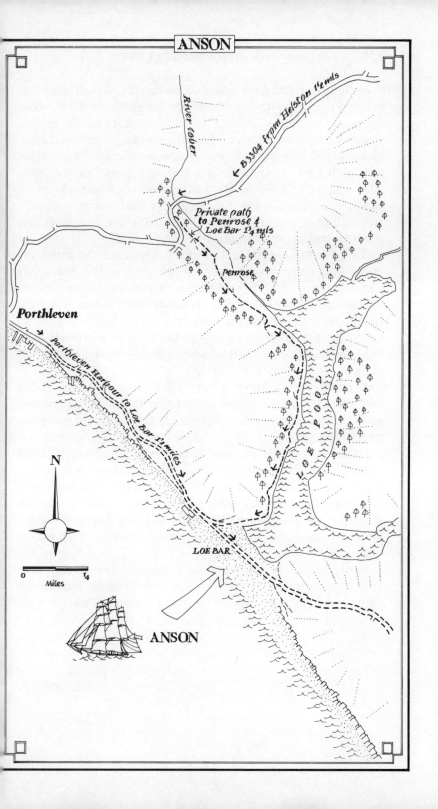

Certainly if you visit the Bar during the sort of gale that brought the *Anson* to her doom, you will have no doubt about the power of the sea there. Giant seas thunder in, the ground shakes beneath your feet, and a dull, booming roar fills the air. The seas crash down, grab and suck at the shingle, and tear out tons with each wave. And then the next giant flings it back. This action of the sea has left a permanent shelf only 25 feet off shore, so just below low tide mark the beach drops suddenly from a foot or two of water to almost 20 feet. It is a dangerous place for bathing or swimming.

To the left of the Bar as you look out to sea on the grassy top of the cliff there is a memorial to the dead of the *Anson* (see picture, Page 125). For the men of the *Anson* are buried somewhere in the cliffs round about the wreck scene. It was the custom in those days to bury the dead on the beaches or on the cliffs where they were found and the cliffs of Cornwall must hold thousands of such unmarked graves. In fact it was not until a year after the loss of the *Anson* that an Act of Parliament was passed – in July 1808 – requiring that bodies cast ashore must be given a Christian burial in consecrated ground. The memorial to the *Anson* dead was erected comparatively recently.

Other evidence of the loss of the *Anson* can be seen in the area. One of her cannon, weighing three-and-a-half tons, and recovered by the Culdrose divers, stands outside Helston Museum. Two of those recovered by Roland Morris serve as gateposts at Porthleven Harbour and he has one at his Penzance museum. Another small one is used to tie up fishing boats at Coverack.

However, before you leave the site of the *Anson's* end, keep your eyes open as you walk over that yielding sand. Who knows, you might find one of Captain Lydiard's coins!

CHAPTER TWELVE

Weazle

The date: February 10th, 1799.
The weather: a great storm in the night, winds strong to gale force westerly, veering north-north-west.

H.M.S. Weazle was about to die in the dark of Barnstaple Bay and with her would die all her crew of 106. And one woman.

But no thought of doom was present at the Saturday night party on board the *Weazle* on February 9th. It was a farewell party, because the *Weazle* was due to sail the next day. And it was a good party. So good, in fact, that many of the inhabitants of Appledore vowed it the best party they had attended in the whole of their lives. Certainly, the Honorable Henry Grey, fourth son of the Earl of Stamford and Warrington, commander of the brig *H.M.S. Weazle*, made sure that all his guests enjoyed themselves. There was no shortage of liquor, some of it confiscated contraband of high quality. For *H.M.S. Weazle* was a brig-of-war engaged in putting down the West Country smuggling traffic, which was in a state of boom at the end of the 18th century.

It is difficult to know just how effective *Weazle* had been for her crew were very popular. So were the smugglers and their cheap goods. So it is possible to imagine that the popularity of the men of the *Weazle* was a sign of a not very successful campaign against "the gentlemen". *Weazle* had used Appledore as her home port for a long time, so that by the night of Captain Grey's party the locals knew them all very well. Now

139

the time had come to part. *Weazle* was ordered to Falmouth and after that only the Lords of the Admiralty knew where they would be sent.

Most of the crew at the party were sad to be leaving. Falmouth discipline was bound to be tougher than that they had been under in Appledore. Not all of the crew were at the party of course. Some were saying goodbye in other ways in darkened rooms in the town. And some would be glad to go before Summer showed the fruits of Winter sowing.

Appledore is about two-and-a-half miles north of Bideford, North Devon at the junction of the Torridge and Taw estuaries, and Captain Grey knew that the large sandbanks would mean that he would have to wait for high tide the next afternoon to take *Weazle* out to sea.

On that Sunday afternoon a large crowd gathered to wave farewell and as the tide filled the estuary, the *Weazle's* boats pulled her gently away from the quay. Once well out in mid-stream, the boats were shipped, sails fluttered from the yards and then filled and took her out to sea. One or two women wept, but soon the ship was indistinct in the gathering gloom. Not all of the darkness was due to the fall of evening. There were storms about.

However, *Weazle* went safely out through the Neck and over the dangerous Barnstaple Bar. Then she turned her port side towards land and headed west towards Hartland Point. We don't know exactly where she was when the storm broke, but she must have been somewhere between Hartland Point and Lundy Island on her way to Falmouth. We know what time it was when the great north-north-west gale came up – somewhere close to 6 p.m. because John James of Bideford on February 17th, 1799 wrote this in a letter to a friend: "She was in the bay that afternoon, and as the people went to church, the seafaring men felt some anxiety, if the wind should shift a point and blow, which it did".

Captain Grey was now in deep trouble, embayed between Lundy Island and the sheer cliffs of Baggy Point to the north of Appledore. Just what desperate manoeuvres he tried, what tacking and running, are all covered by the dark, but slowly he

15   A model of *H.M.S. Alert*, sister ship to the *Weazle*

was forced to the north and all the time was driven closer and closer in to the shore. Just before midnight, the *Weazle* fired her guns as a signal of distress, but there was nothing anyone who heard them could do to help. The distress guns went on at intervals until one in the morning. And then suddenly ceased. The *Weazle* had ploughed into the rocks of Baggy Point and the rest was silence.

Writing to report the wreck, Philip Rogers Webber, Lord of the Manor of Croyde noted: "On the tenth instant off Morte Bay Guns of distress was heard from a ship which ceased at one o'clock. At five in the morning a wreck was discovered on the Sands which proved to be His Majesty's Ship Weazel. Great part of her upperworks and Boats all to pieces".

The Sands he refers to are the popular surfing beaches of today's Croyde Bay which are backed by high sandhills.

And we know from that other letter of the time, from John James, that after the wreck they were lined with people ... "That fine ship perished and as yet only one body has been taken up, but many are watching from opposite the beach, both yesterday and today, and are fishing up fragments of the wreck. We have since heard that the wreck is visible at low water, this side of Baggy Point".

We know too that the first body to be washed up was that of a woman. But we'll come to the reason for that shortly.

Not all the crew of the *Weazle* died. In fact one man missed the ship's sailing and it is tempting to think that he had such a good farewell party that he only awoke after the ship had sailed. Or maybe he stayed too long a-bed in some Appledore lady's arms. The ship's purser, Simon Haly, too, was not on board. He was ashore sick. Letters telling us this can still be seen today in the Public Record Office, though, sadly, they do not mention the reason for the seaman missing the ship. It is interesting to note too that in those same records two of the seamen lost are marked as having joined on the same day, August 20th, 1798 and both came from America.

Whether they were "refugees" from the Declaration of Independence of the former American colonies or whether enough time had passed for the complete acceptance of

America as another independent state, it is impossible to say, but Robert Brown is marked as "N. American" and Owen Jones as "America" in the last surviving paybook of the ship.

It was, however, weeks before another body was washed up. This time it was that of the Surgeon, William Grey, who was no relation of the Captain. All told only 24 bodies were ever found, one of the last being that of the ship's Lieutenant W.C. Butler, of whose body it was said that it was, apart from damage to his face, in "as perfect a state as if he had only just drowned" - and that was a full three months after the wreck.

The loss of the *Weazle* upset the good citizens of Appledore and their grief appears quite genuine. A full funeral service was held in Bideford and was packed with mourners from miles around. Poems were written:

> "The tale is briefly told:— a gallant bark
> Embayed, and by the tempest overtaken,
> When midnight heavens were glooming pitchy dark,
> And wave and shore by the loud storm were shaken,
> Drove upon Baggy's horrid Leap - and hark!
> The seaman's cry, that never more shall waken
> Echo for mirth or woe:— down-down she goes,
> And for her fate a long Lament arose".

The Lament, which follows, was well enough preserved locally for it to be published in the North Devon Magazine, The Cave, in March, 1824:

> "Lament for the WEAZLE,
>   The joy of our Bay;
> Whose trim was so gallant,
>   Whose crew were so gay;
> Hearts that never knew fear,
>   Yet confess'd beauty's eye, —
> Then rain beauty's tear,
>   For the day-dream gone by!

Lament for the WEAZLE,
　The grace of our POOL;
　O! where is her sceptre
　Of wide-ocean rule?
The waves in their madness
　To freedom awoke,
And the Sea-queen o'erwhelmed
　As her sceptre they broke.

Lament for the WEAZLE,
　Her voyages are o'er;
She hath made her last port,
　She is on her lee-shore;
Low down in the deep,
　When the sunbeams are sheen,
And the waters are calm,
　May her ruins be seen.

Hope breathed on her sail,
　As she went o'er the Bar;
Pride waved in her ensign,
　Seen flying from afar;
But her sail it was struck
　Ere the Bay she had crost,
Her ensign was lowered —
　Her glory was lost.

Tho' the tear fell at parting,
　When love bade adieu,
There was "welcome to ocean!"
　From all her bold CREW,
And the wine-cup was spilt,
　As it circled her deck,
But the blood of the gay
　Is now red on her wreck.

Who hath escaped
　From the tempest's fell sweep,
From the crush of her timbers
　On BAGGY's dark LEAP?
Not a soul:— there was one
　Left behind on the shore,
His fortune to thank,
　But his FRIENDS to deplore.

> Comrades in danger,
>   Companions in mirth,
> Some sleep their last sleep
>   In a watery berth,
> And on whom the tide
>   Hath restored as it rose,
> By BRAUNTON'S grove-altar
>   Is gone to repose.
>
> Lament for the WEAZLE,
>   Her voyages are o'er,
> From the port she last made
>   Came their ship never more:
> And tho' memory long
>   Our LAMENT will renew,
> Fill it up! - but in silence —
>   A glass to her CREW!"

The lament for the *Weazle* is extraordinary in that it commemorates the death of quite a small ship by Navy standards. The *Weazle* was one of eight sloops built after 1775. It is difficult to know exactly what to call her as she was at times referred to as a Brig, a Sloop, and sometimes as a Brigantine.

If you want to know what she looked like there is a model of her sister ship, *H.M.S. Alert* in the Science Museum, London.

Weazle was just one inch short of 79 feet long and had a beam of 25 feet, tonnage 201. She was built at Sandwich, Kent and launched on April 18th, 1783. She was armed with twelve 4-pounder cannon and sixteen half-pound swivel guns. She was small, but fast and easily handled, though there was little room or comfort (the headroom between decks being only 5 feet) for the 106 men who crewed her.

Which brings us to the woman aboard, whom local tradition names as one Nancy Golding. It may well be that Captain Grey had no idea that a woman was still aboard when he sailed, but there are records of women emerging from all sorts of hidey-holes below decks of other ships during a battle and tending the wounded or serving the guns beside their men. But officially no woman was allowed on board unless she was the genuine wife of a seaman. This was not strictly enforced and most women on board were common prostitutes. What Nancy was no one can say, but if she was a stowaway she certainly paid dearly for it.

How to get there

To find the *Weazle's* grave you have to go first of all to that area of North Devon which is renowned for wonderful stretches of clean sand and surfing, the sea-shores south of Ilfracombe.

For those who like a long walk a good starting out point is Woolacombe. To your left are two miles of wonderful sands. There are extensive car-parks behind the sand-hills which overlook the beach. The headland at the far, southern, end is Baggy Point which, together with the headland of Morte Point on your right, form the claws of a great trap for the sailing ships of long ago. Many ships have been embayed and wrecked in the waters before you, hence the name of Morte (or Death) Point. This headland is criss-crossed with paths along which it is said wreckers drove cattle with lanterns tied to their horns to lure ships ashore. You can take that with a pinch of salt, but it is true that the headland did often turn out to be Death Point for old-time sailors.

Baggy Point is easily reached from the hamlet of Putsborough and paths lead you right around the two-mile long, half-mile wide headland. The cliffs are sheer and dangerous so take care.

Do not lean over even if you spot seals on the rocks below. They are often to be seen on the rocks near the caves which are numerous. At the highest point the cliffs, which are National Trust property, are over 300 feet above sea level. At the

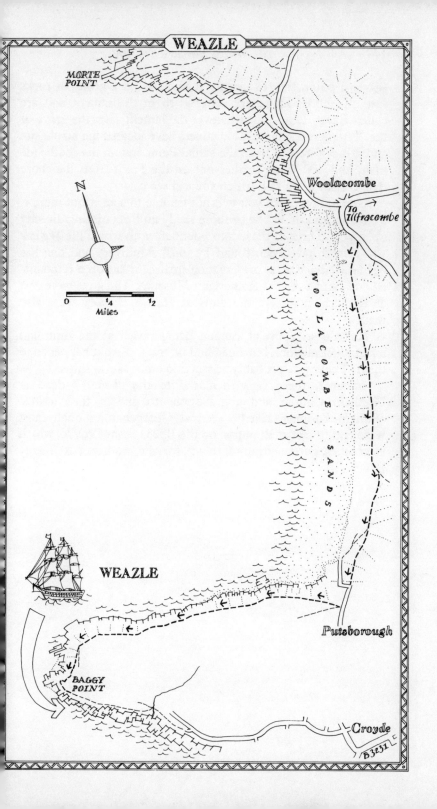

seaward point, the sea usually foams around a group of rocks just off shore. These are referred to in the lament and are called Baggy Leap. But whatever the lament says, the grave of the *Weazle* is not there. Skin-divers have located the actual site and it is 500 feet in from the actual Point and on the south side of it, and 400 yards further out on the Point from the shore than the sewer outfall, which you can see clearly.

As you look down you will not be able to spot it but there is a cannon muzzle in one of those sandy gullies pointing directly up at you. Three of those four pounders with which the *Weazle* was armed have been found by local skindivers and one has been raised and after preservation treatment has been remounted and can be seen at Rotherham Museum. The guns were cast at Rotherham, where the guns of *H.M.S. Victory* were also made.

There is a report of cannon being raised at the time and taken to Appledore, but I can find no trace of what happened to them. They were probably reissued to other Naval ships.

However, there is a memorial to the *Weazle's* dead at Northam Church and a gravestone to one of the victims, William Kidman, can be seen at Georgeham, though most were laid to rest at Braunton on the B3231 from Croyde, which is another good setting-off place for the walk out to Baggy Point.